The Race for the Championship

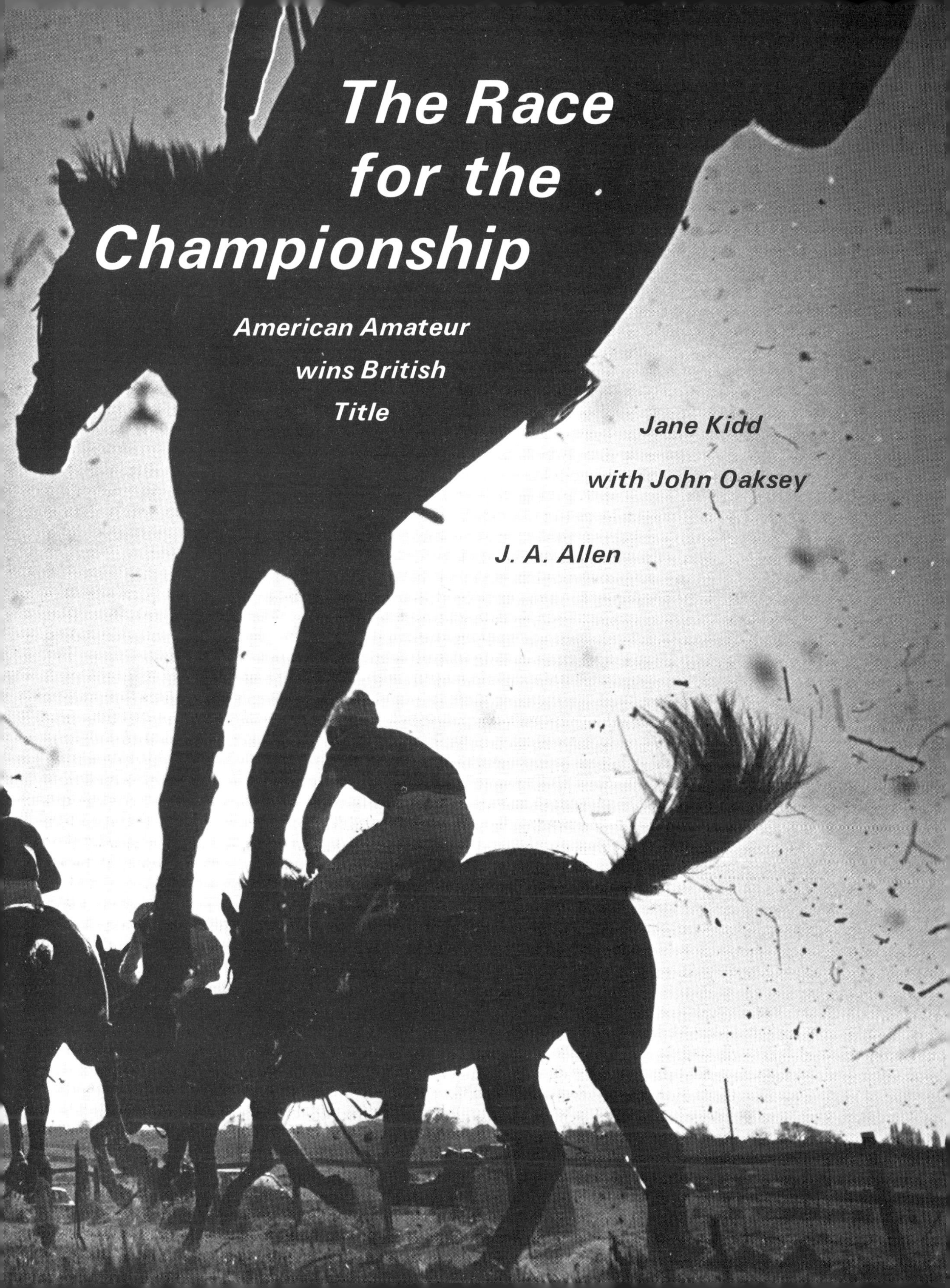

The Race for the Championship

American Amateur wins British Title

Jane Kidd

with John Oaksey

J. A. Allen

First published 1979 by J. A. Allen & Co Ltd
1 Lower Grosvenor Place, Buckingham Palace Road, London SW1W 0EL
ISBN 0 85131 325 6

Produced by The Compton Press Ltd
The Old Brewery, Tisbury, Wiltshire
Designed by Jonathan Tetley

Filmset by BAS Printers Limited
Over Wallop, Hampshire
Colour Plates and Jacket printed by C. H. Woodward Ltd
Devizes, Wiltshire
Bound by J. M. Dent & Sons Ltd
Letchworth, Hertfordshire

Photographic Acknowledgements

Eric Buston & Associates, page 27; Bill Cain, 19, 34; *Courier-Journal and Louisville Times*, 16; Findlay Davidson, 22; David Ellis, 32 (*upper*), 64, 65 *and colour picture of Tiepolino* (between pp. 48–49); Fox Photos, 6; Douglas Lees, 35 (*upper*); Frank H. Meads, 59, 60; Jim Meads, 84, 86; *Nashville Banner*, 19; *The Nashville Tennesseean*, 17, 20–21; Les Nelson, 13; Bernard Parkin, 1, 2, 3, 8, 9; Selwyn Photos, 5, 10, 29, 31, 56–57, 58, 77, 80–81; *The Tennesseean*, 32 (*lower*), 35 (*lower*), 36, 37, 38; Susie Thomas, 23.

Contents

The author of this chapter, John Oaksey, on one of the best horses he rode, Taxidermist.

1 The Aura of the Championship

When you are sitting on a horse with no very obvious chance at the start of an unimportant novice steeplechase round, say, Plumpton or Fontwell Park – with your heart somewhere between your mouth and your boots and your fingers stiffening with nerves and cold on sweaty reins – it is sometimes quite hard, I seem to remember, to persuade yourself that you are really doing all this for fun.

But the word 'amateur' does derive from the latin verb to love – *amo, amas, amat* and all that – and I once heard Paul Mellon remind his audience at Mill Reef's Gimcrack Dinner that an amateur of anything is – or should be – someone who does that thing because he loves it. I have to admit that Mr Mellon added 'just as many lovers know precious little about love, amateurs often know precious little about anything'. I can think of quite a few professional jockeys who would agree wholeheartedly, but that is by the way.

The fact remains that in steeplechasing much of the word's original meaning has survived. In that imaginary race at Plumpton, for instance, if your horse just happens to meet the first few fences right, if he stands back when you ask him and gets a length or two and then, best of all, if he quickens away from the last and somehow finishes in front, it seems entirely reasonable to count yourself in love with the sensations he has given you. All those black doubts and fears will have been swept behind you as quickly as the fences and as you ride back, hot, breathless and blissfully happy the question is not so much 'why am I doing this?', as 'where the devil can I find anything else on earth to give me such a thrill?'.

People have probably been asking that question in one form or another ever since men first tried asking horses to jump. It has certainly been asked pretty regularly in the British Isles since 1739 when two Irish sportsmen called Blake and O'Calloghan set off to ride across country from Buttevant Church to St Leger steeple. No one seems to know who won that first recorded 'steeplechase', but even if there were a few side bets involved it has never been suggested that Messrs Blake and O'Calloghan were doing it principally for money. They simply wanted to test themselves, and their horses and, win, lose or fall, they fully expected to enjoy it.

The spirit which inspired those cheerful pioneers has been operating ever since and, even

Ian Balding (champion 1962–63) on Caduval.

if its results now look a bit more organized and regulated than Messrs B and C's impromptu frolic, the spirit itself is still alive and flourishing in the 20th century. For well over 200 years it has been causing men and women to do eccentric, improbable, sometimes hazardous things – and in 1977 it brought George Sloan across the Atlantic in search of the Bollinger Trophy.

To understand what George was after you must first understand the peculiar place which amateurs and amateur riding still holds in British jumping.

Historically, as we have seen, amateur foxhunting men can fairly claim to have started it all but for more than a century now jumping has been a largely professional partner and counterpart of flat racing. It is still, regrettably, allowed only a fraction of the prize money which is available, for far less effort, on the flat – but, 'poor relation' or not there are still many thousands to whom, whether they take part or merely watch, the thrill and spectacle of jumping means far more than all the million-dollar glamour of the flat.

Macer Gifford (champion 1964–65) winning at Cheltenham on Larbawn. The same combination won the Whitbread Gold Cup.

Richard Tate (champion 1967–68 and 1968–69) on Wedding Dance.

Michael Dickinson (champion 1969–70) wins at Stratford on Shirlath.

Although the Jockey Club rules by which both jumping and flat racing are controlled were often originally drawn up and are now enforced by men who themselves came into racing as amateur riders they are, quite rightly, designed to protect the professional jockey who makes his living from the sport. This 'protection' has inevitably made life harder for the amateur but only the foolish and ignorant complain because it is all too obvious that a professional has little enough chance to earn a decent living without having to worry about competition from unpaid 'gentlemen' who are doing it for fun.

Nowadays in fact, there are two forms of amateur permit and until he has shown a certain minimum degree of competence an amateur is only given an 'A' permit which allows him to ride in confined amateur races, hunter chases and of course point-to-points – though point-to-points do not count towards the amateur riders' title. Once you ride a winner or otherwise demonstrate that you are no longer an uncontrolled danger to the navigation of your opponents, you get a full 'B' permit and are qualified to ride in any race for which someone is rash or kind enough to put you up. But after a total of only 75 rides against professionals any such owner has to pay the full riding fee into a central administrative fund. It is fairly self-evident that no one in his senses is going to pay twice over for the services of an amateur so I think it can be said without much fear of contradiction that the 'shamateur' who not only competes unfairly with professionals but also sets out to make money in the process is a thing of the past.

The amateur, however, is not. More than 500 men and women were granted permits to ride in 1977/78 and heaven knows how many more rode in point-to-points for which no Jockey Club permit is required. So what are the motives which inspire them?

For the reasons given above money is clearly not among them and for much the same reason it is no longer necessarily true – as it once almost certainly was – that anyone aiming to become a professional jumping jockey is best advised if possible to start as an amateur. Those 75 'free' rides are still some help in that direction but until the late 1950s no limitation of any kind was put on an amateur so long as he persuaded the stewards that he was not earning his living from riding. Not having to pay your jockey a fee was inevitably a powerful incentive to some owners to use amateurs and although I do not suggest that there was anything undeserved about their success, the fact is that seven post-war champion jockeys did start with a 'Mr' in front of their name. No one, since the war, has actually headed both the professional and the amateur lists but 9 leading amateurs have turned professional, most of them with considerable success. Of course others may follow them – if only because there are, alas, fewer and fewer men or women who can afford to ride at all regularly without getting even their expenses paid. (I only managed to do it myself by writing for the newspapers about racing but there are unfortunately not enough jobs to make that a very common subterfuge.)

But there is still no shortage whatsoever of would-be amateurs and although, of course, no two are exactly the same I believe that their motives can be grouped under three main headings – enjoyment, fellowship and tradition. These admittedly are blanket, coverall sort of words – so let me try to explain what I mean.

Well, first, of course, come the sensations I have already tried to describe – the mouth-drying nerves beforehand and the glorious exhilaration when things go even halfway right. I don't believe anyone has ever set out seriously to learn to ride as an amateur who had not, at some stage – whether out hunting or in a pony club gymkhana or wherever – felt and enjoyed the sensation of getting from one side of an obstacle to the other on horseback; either you like it or you don't. If you do like it, the pleasure and thrill you get is apt to be very considerably magnified by doing it again and again at 30 mph surrounded by 10 or 20 others who are trying to do the same thing, only better.

Of course there is also the other side of the coin – the falls and bruises and occasional broken bones, the bitterness of failure and the shame of making yourself look foolish through your own unfitness, stupidity or incompetence.

All these are part of the second heading 'fellowship' – by which I mean the pleasure of making yourself a part, however insignificant and unimportant, of a unique sport which is also, for one extraordinary group of men, a way of life.

Until the 'A' and 'B' permit system was introduced it was, in theory, quite possible for a beardless unschooled amateur to find himself in the very first race of his 'career' rubbing knees at the start with men like Fred Winter, Jonjo O'Neill or John Francome. And even now, granted the right horse or the money to buy him, you only need minimal experience to compete against the best. Understandably the best themselves may not like that much but, in fact, inexperienced professionals are just as dangerous as inexperienced amateurs and both just have to be faced among the other hazards of the game.

'The only thing I ever tell an amateur is to get out of my bloody way', David Mould was once quoted as saying. Even if that had been true (which it certainly wasn't) he would have been an exception to the general rule.

Amateur rider John Edwards takes a spectacular fall.

Professional-amateur rivalry exists all right but 'the ground feels the same to everyone when you hit it' is a much more typical attitude. Once an amateur proves himself a trier – someone who, however unsuccessful, is at least genuinely doing his best to learn the game, he will soon find himself accepted at his worth – not quite like a fellow professional, perhaps, but at least as someone who has earned his right to a place in the changing room. And that, as any retired jockey, professional or amateur, will tell you, is the warmest, friendliest, most cheerful place on a racecourse. One thing every jockey misses most when he hangs up his boots for good is the right to sit in that dirty, smelly, untidy crowded room. When you first enter it, dumb with nerves, ill-equipped and totally ignorant of what you are meant to do next, the chaotic jumble of busy valets, muddy tack and sweating shouting half-changed jockeys looks and sounds like some nightmare corner of hell. But quite soon as you get accustomed to the complex routine of changing and weighing out that hell becomes the nearest thing to home a racecourse has to offer – a comforting haven where you can find friendship and sympathy and the cheerful comradeship of dangers shared.

Lord Mildmay riding at Kempton Park in 1949.

What happens on the racecourse, needless to say, is only part of the life and only part of its pleasure. Anyone riding at all regularly – particularly if he wants to get even halfway fit – must also get used to the crack-of-dawn routine of a training stable, to the misery of rain on a biting wind and the glory of clear blue days high on lonely downs when the horse you are riding feels like Arkle and you feel lucky to be alive.

But why do it all as an amateur? Why not get paid for doing what you love so much? Well, first of all there are already far too many professional jockeys for all of them to earn even the start of a living. Only an exceptional amateur could hope to break into the charmed circle at or anywhere near the top – and at least if you do not turn professional you have chances of rides in hunters chases and in all the other races confined to amateurs.

For some at least tradition is also part of the answer – the proud tradition which Blake and O'Calloghan founded, which men like Captain Becher and Squire Osbaldeston carried on – and which is by no means dead even in the second half of this mechanical, electronic century. It is 60 years since Harry Brown became the last amateur to head both lists as champion jockey. Like Captain Becher (who could imitate almost every known animal and used to jump on to mantelpieces after dinner) Brown was a first-rate all round sportsman. Once, arriving early at Chepstow Races he backed himself to ride a winner and catch the biggest salmon of the season in the same afternoon. He duly caught the salmon but then his beloved Dudley, usually a model of reliability, spoilt the double by falling at the last fence.

Between the wars, amateur riding flourished notably in the Army, which still had horses in those happy days. Obviously they have gone now, but since the war, even if the general military standard has inevitably fallen, the tradition has survived mechanization and inflation.

Amateur riding's greatest upholder in this century – perhaps in any century – was surely the late Lord Mildmay who reigned as leading amateur for five years from the end of the Second World War until his tragic death by drowning. This almost certainly resulted from the same neck injury which three years earlier had brought about the second of his tragic and luckless near-misses in the Grand National. The first on Davy Jones was caused by an unbuckled rein and then, riding Cromwell in 1948, Lord Mildmay suffered such cramp in his neck that, unable to raise his head, he had to ride virtually blind over the last half-dozen fences – to finish third, only beaten seven lengths. Universally popular with the racing public, Anthony Mildmay was also a friend and companion-in-arms to all professionals with whom he rode. He used often to act as a steward even at meetings where he was riding and once, round the final turn at Newton Abbot heard an agonized cry from behind him – 'for God's sake go on my Lord, this one isn't wanted today'. 'My lord' did indeed go on to win and needless to say 'forgot' the incident as soon as he dismounted.

After his death a leading article in *The Times* described the amateur tradition as he embodied it far better than I could hope to do.

'There never was a harder rider, a better loser or a more popular winner; and although he always valued the race more than the victory and the victory more than the prize, he would not perhaps have disdained the reward he has won – which is a kind of immortality among the English'.

Such men, alas, come rarely and nowadays it is desperately difficult for anyone to afford as many of his own horses in training as Lord Mildmay kept at Fairlawne with his lifelong friend Peter Cazalet. Nevertheless the tradition has been maintained.

Certainly no amateur since the war suffered more injuries and broken bones than Gay

Sir William Pigott-Brown winning on Superfine.

Chris Collins (champion 1965–66 and 1966–67) winning the Horse & Hound Cup on Santa Grande.

Kindersley who headed the list in 1959/60. He was followed by William Pigott-Brown who came into the game looking like a chubby schoolboy and left it four years later after twice becoming leading amateur, mostly on his own or his family's horses. The most skilful amateurs to ride in this country in my memory have I believe been Alan Lillingston (the only one to win a Champion Hurdle) and Bob McCreery who, till injuries cut short his career, could hold his own with all but the very best professionals.

Chris Collins may never quite have attained that level of ability but his has, in its way, been the most extraordinary career of any post war leading amateur. Born the wrong shape – far too long and a good deal too heavy – he decided in the early 1960s that what he wanted most was to succeed as an amateur and, if possible, head the list. At the time I remember thinking his prospects remote and his father thought even less of Chris's chance in the chartered accountants' examination for which he was sitting at the time.

We were both proved completely and comprehensively wrong. Chris bet his father a large

Bob McCreery on Pride of Ivanhoe.

sum of money at handsome odds that he would finish in the first six in that highly competitive accountancy exam. Having won the bet he used the money to start buying a string of good horses on which, trained by Arthur Stephenson he proceeded to ride to two amateur championships. Until George Sloan came along no one had ever planned and carried through a campaign to take the amateur title with more skill, attention to detail and, needless to say, the courage and dash without which the title has never been won.

This then is the tradition to which I refer. It explains not only why so many take so much trouble to ride as amateurs but also why it seems to so many of them so infinitely well worthwhile to strain every nerve for 11 months of the year, to travel up and down the country (or in George Sloan's case round the world) in search of rides. If it is worth being an amateur then your ambition is inevitably to be leading amateur. It is a worthy ambition and if people ever stop trying to achieve it, the whole sport will be very much the poorer.

Peter Greenall (champion 1975–76 and 1976–77) winning on Timmie's Battle.

Prime Motive, George's best horse in America.

The 1969 Grand National with George on the grey Peccard falling at Becher's.

2 The Dream

Before we learned the story
Writ down by racing feet
He taught us all the glory
The long years would repeat.
W. H. OGILVIE

What makes a person leave a successful business, a lovely home, a stableful of racehorses and hunters in order to risk a great deal of money, time and health on racing after the Amateur title? He has to be whimsical enough to dream, daring enough to try, and determined enough to make those dreams work.

George Sloan was brought up to dream about earning glory in the hunting field, on the racecourse and at business. His dream maker was Mason Houghland, Master of the local Foxhounds, the Hillsboro, a business magnate who ran a chain of petrol stations, but who in his youth had made and lost a fortune as an oil wild catter. Houghland was a great story teller and a lucid writer on foxhunting.

As early as five years old George became the protégé of Mason Houghland, who must have seen flickerings of a kindred spirit of adventure in this son of John Sloan, his co-founder of the Hillsboro Hounds. For the following 14 years until his death in 1959, Houghland had George agog with the thrills of working with the hounds, racing over steeplechase fences and of earning enough money to do these sports well.

George's childhood helped to fire the spirits of an adventurer. At home he was one of four

Mason Houghland telling a story to George and his brother John.

An early taste of hunting at just three years old.

sons to whom a little devilment, a good smattering of pranks and mischief were necessary ingredients to life. With Mason Houghland he even missed school to go hunting, to ride alongside his hero and listen to stories that made him dream that paradise lay over the next hill. These nurtured young George Sloan's ambitions, making him eager to seek out adventures that would lead him over the hills to glory.

He started with a 'hill' close to home, and that was to win the greatest annual equestrian event in his home town of Nashville. This was the three-mile Iroquois steeplechase named after Nashville's most famous equine resident who in 1881 became the first American winner of the British Derby.

Whereas the rest of the world might be under the impression that the only important activity in Nashville is the strumming of guitar strings and the recording of the world's best country singers, the locals themselves would also mention the Iroquois Hunt Meeting. For a week or more every May Nashville conversation and newpapers centre round horses, as well as what to wear, or was worn, at the innumerable cocktail parties, dinners, balls and breakfasts that precede and follow the more sporting activities on the racecourse in Warner Park. The Iroquois Hunt meeting has become one of the city's most publicized and social occasions of the year.

With this background of parties, the 10,000 or more people who go to the races are in pretty high spirits. Although they are not allowed to risk raising or destroying their good humour with a bet on the horses – gambling is banned in Tennessee – they can get plenty of entertainment through the variety of races. The children run in pony races, the ladies in a flat race, and there is also one for the gentlemen. Then there is a timber race and three steeplechases over some of the few permanent fences still used in the country where plastic fences are the rule.

The 'well to do' Nashvillians buy enclosures for $100 a go, giving them the right to six seats and a few square feet of the grassland. The Southerners' overwhelming appreciation of success and capacity for turning their particular activity into the greatest thing that ever happended means the victors earn themselves plenty of glory; but the hero of the day is the winner of one of the few three-mile chases in America, the Iroquois. For him there is such publicity, celebrations and local fame that his prestige rating within Nashville and the surrounding Tennessee is as good as the winner of the Cheltenham Gold Cup in England.

George clear of the field in the 1950 pony race at the Iroquois meeting.

George had early tastes of minor glories at the meeting when as a 9, 10 and 11 year-old he won the pony race on an Arab cross thoroughbred runt. He made the step to a horse for the Iroquois when he was 15 years-old, but the horse his father bought for him took four months of the preparatory work only to break down just before the race. The same frustrating sequence of events happened the following year – an early tempering of the steel required to face the ups and downs of a steeplechase rider.

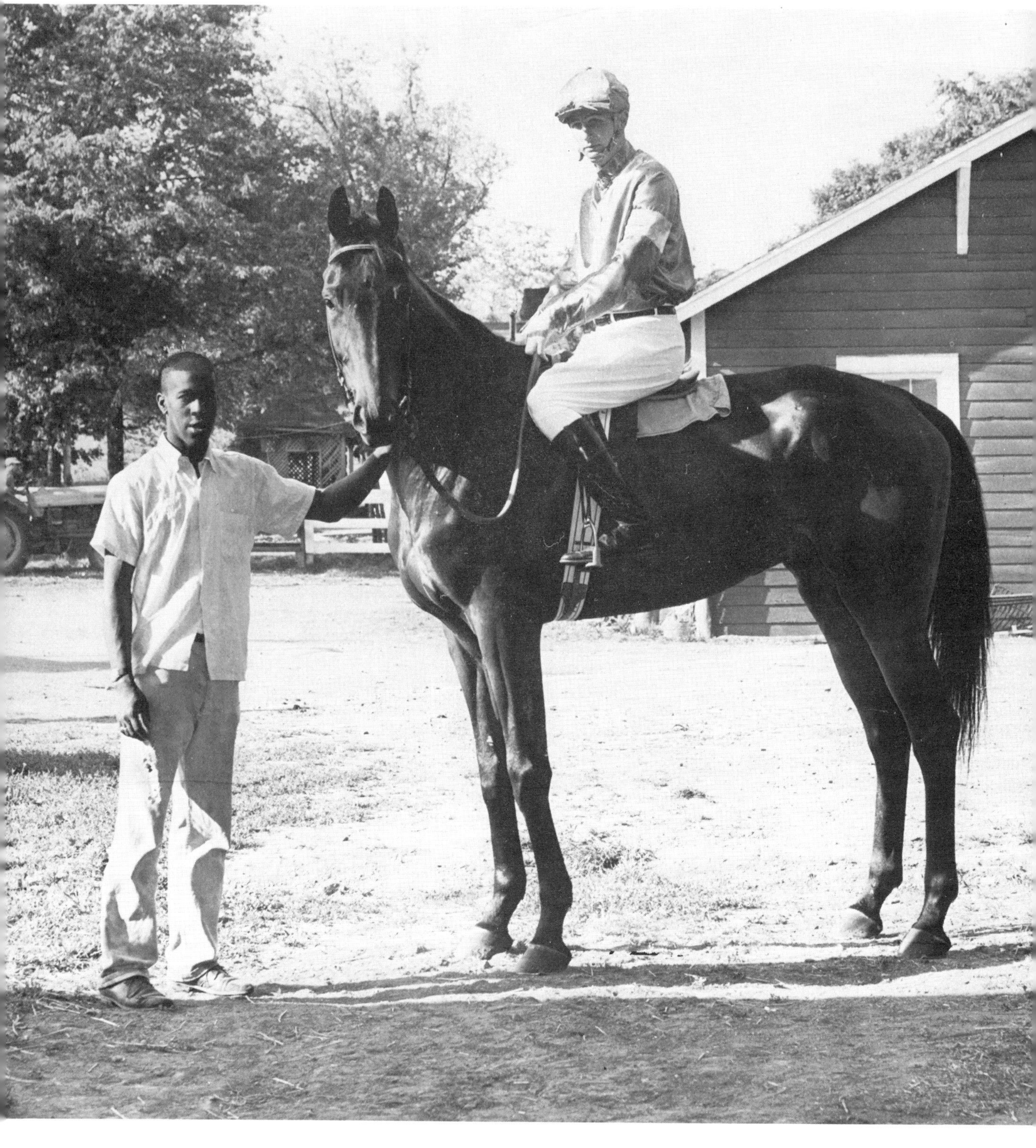

That tempering continued for when 17 years-old he made the start of the race, but not the finish as the horse fell; the next time was more ignominious as he got 'jumped off' the favourite; and the third was more painful as he was offered a spare ride at the last moment, but not having ridden for six months he was in agony for the last mile of the race and the following two weeks. Then in 1961, when 21 years-old, he made it. George became the local hero, the winner of the Iroquois.

This Iroquois success fired George's love of racing and perhaps if it had happened a little earlier it would have persuaded him in favour of the career he hankered after, becoming a professional jockey. As it was, after three years of unconventional activities he had returned to the 'Establishment' way of life – studying at Vanderbilt University – when the triumph finally came.

If victory had come in the year he had discarded student life at Cornell University to return home and hunt the hounds full-time and go to school part-time, things might have been different. Even during the two years he had supervised the building and organization of a chain of filling stations, he still might have followed the 'irrational' career of a professional rider. But at 20 years of age he had married Mason Houghland's granddaughter. The responsibilities of this step and the need to assert his independence – with his boss now being his father-in-law – persuaded George to return to the grind of intellectual studies. He hoped it would prove to be the best way of following his mentor Mason Houghland's advice that a chief satisfaction in sports is to earn the money to do them well.

Local Run, George's first winner of the Iroquois.

George qualified in law at Vanderbilt University, practised corporate law, and took his first major business plunge in 1967 buying franchises for Mini-Pearl Fried Chicken. He built up a chain of these chicken stores in the South and when the going appeared very good in 1969, he sold the franchise, the real estate, and most of the stock in the parent company, whose shares had risen from 50 cents to $60 in eight months. He had made himself financially independent and able to go racing where he wanted.

These years spent building up the business had not been devoid of racing. He had been riding horses for Nashvillian friends – Calvin Houghland, Rhodes Hart, Paul Banks, Vernon Sharp, William Tyne and Henry Hooker. George could not rely on money or luck for the rides he dearly wanted; so, with some cheek, and even agression, he managed to persuade them that it would be fun to own horses, hire a trainer, and run a centre with himself as stable jockey. He made it fun too, riding horses to win another Iroquois, an Oxmoor, numerous point-to-points and enough races to make him twice the runner-up for the American Amateur title.

By 1970, George had the finance, and the freedom from the traumas of building up a business to concentrate on racing. This was the year to climb 'hill' number two, the American Amateur Steeplechase title. He had 10 horses to ride, owned by himself and his father-in law Calvin Houghland, and he sent them wherever they were eligible and capable of running. It entailed thousands of miles of travelling to get just 34 rides as most of America's meetings are concentrated a long way away in the East and are only staged on weekends in the spring and autumn. The Southerners were better known for showing off the spectacular gaits of the Tennessee Walkers than galloping over fences.

The South does, however, stage the first meetings of the season in March and early April. Tryon was one of these, a hilly racecourse lying in North Carolina in the foothills of the Blue Ridge mountains. It was here that George won his first race of the year, a timber race over solid fences – a form of racing thought more appropriate to foolhardy amateurs than wary and battle-scarred professionals. As a rule, only gentlemen riders race over these adaptations of the fences which the pioneers built to divide their property and the early foxhunters chased over. These obstacles can be sloping and only 3 ft 6 in high; but those are the easiest. They rise in height and difficulty to the extreme of the Maryland Hunt Cup where they are upright and the highest a fearsome 5 ft 2 in of solid wood panel. Only a courageous jockey and a clever horse could take on these fences at speed.

The Tryon was the beginning and the end of George's timber racing season due to that most frequent of racing catastrophies – his horse broke down. He now had to concentrate on the horses that did not jump so high but galloped faster. He had the material to do this for at Lexington he took a flat and brush race. He did

A timber race at the Oxmoor meeting with George on one of his best horses, Bongocero.

The 1970 Iroquois.

even better at his home meeting in Nashville for he won all three brush races including the illustrious Iroquois for the third time. It made his 'double' two weeks later at the end of May Oxmoor meeting seem almost run of the mill.

In June, American steeplechasing moves to the major tracks and loses its sporting intimacy. At these the prize money is plentiful but the horse is merely a means to the end of betting. The jumpers are treated as amusing but annoying creatures because of their habit of falling makes them a risky betting medium.

In George's year the main tracks incorporating a jump race amongst their nine or more races four or five times a week were Saratoga, Aqueduct and Delaware and horses were left to

Somaten wins the Iroquois in 1970, the year George was America's Champion Amateur.

George carries the 1970 Iroquois trophy.

train at these for the duration of a meeting (a month or more). It was all very commercial, mechanical and hardly a place for a sporting amateur, but George was determined to have a go anywhere that could help him on his way to the Championship. He sent north his triple novice winner Dinner Jacket to try out both Aqueduct and Delaware but there was no glory; that all went in 1970 to the flying Tingle Creek who only showed his backside to the other novices.

An amateur's prospects improve again in September when steeplechasing's forum switches back to the more sporting and colourful hunt meetings. There is one nearly every weekend through to the most lucrative and only international prize of the year, the Colonial Cup in November. George kept trying in 1970, kept travelling but did not manage a single win. The seconds and thirds accumulated but not the victories. In the end, it did not matter, nobody caught his spring total and he emerged the Amateur Champion of 1970.

The 31 year-old amateur rider was a happy man. For so long he had to fight against that dream of becoming a 'pro', but at last he had his reward. He had also avoided the prospect that faces so many professionals – having to look down the gun-barrel of what to do with no qualifications?

With no such worries, George Sloan was after more hills; and he had spotted one a couple of years before he lifted the title in America. He had gone to the UK and discovered that he could pursue his passion for going flat out over fences much more frequently than in the USA. British amateurs got more rides than a professional did in the States, with nearly 500 meetings in the year to America's 30-odd hunt meets and three or four major track meetings. The British rides too were over stiffer fences which suited the daredevil spirit of this American hungry for challenges. Also to his taste were the number of people who felt like he did about steeplechasing; they wanted to do it or even watch it, not for any financial returns but because they loved it.

Most provoking of all, his first ventures in the UK had been fairly disastrous. He had not been recognized as a talented amateur from the States, but as a foolhardy rich Southerner who bought the wrong horses and could not ride them as the professionals had done. George Sloan had fallen down that hill and it had left him smarting.

George weighing out for the 1971 Colonial Cup.

This venture into UK racing started when his youngest brother Paul set off to broaden his horizons by teaching for a year at Lancing College in Sussex. True to Sloan family tradition he was a hunting/racing man and soon tired of the school's sports as they did not include horses.

Driving through the West Sussex village of Findon, Paul saw a sign to 'the Pony Farm', followed it but went down the adjoining drive. He did not realized his mistake as this led into a stable yard. Paul asked the first person he saw, 'Can I get a ride at this pony farm'? Ron James, head lad for the five-times champion National Hunt trainer Ryan Price was taken aback, but short of jockeys to ride out he questioned Paul about his riding background and legged him up on to a huge English 'chaser. Paul decided these were 'mighty fine ponies', and came every morning he was not needed at school. It took Ryan Price a couple of weeks to realize there was a Southerner in the midst of his string, but it did

Paul Sloan falls, bringing down others, at the 1965 Iroquois meeting.

not take the Findon maestro as long to realize that here was potential ownership material.

A few days later, Paul was on the telephone to the keenest race rider in the family 'Say George I found a place where we could get a couple of horses for the Grand National'.

George, who had not ridden in a race since a bad dose of concussion in the spring and had again become submerged in the business of making money, recognized this as his type of adventure. 'That sounds just fine to me,' was the cool reply, but the humdrum Southern drawl disguised the sparks that were flying at the thought of riding in the greatest race in the world.

The Sloan brothers George and Paul walk out to their first British race at Kempton followed by their trainer Ryan Price.

In December, he set off on this the first of innumerable trips across the Atlantic, but it was not a rewarding introduction to British racing for the tracks froze and all sport was abandoned. The next trip was even more disheartening, for three weeks the country was on the verge of thawing out, three times he was publicized as being on a favourite, but not once did he start. The lack of racing gave George time to build up his British horsepower, but despite accumulating eight mounts he only made the racetrack five times. One of these visits, however, was successful.

It was at Folkestone where he and Noble Spirit just got up to win a hurdle race from the leading jockey Terry Biddlecombe, and a field of 28. Here was a new type of glory for the American to beat so many horses – in the States there were never more than 14 – and to become part of that racecourse euphoria that enhanced the thrill of victory. The winner's enclosure; the presentation of the trophy; the press's eager questioning; the congratulations; and the champagne – all so special, so extravagant that it seemed hardly possible that five other groups of people at Folkestone – not to mention a further 18 at the other two race meetings – were enjoying the same ritual. Over the years, the English racing folk have made winning a much greater thrill than in any other country.

It was just as well to have this good feeling buoying up spirits when George went to face the 1969 National. He was to ride a horse called Peccard that was too small for a tall man, and too difficult for an amateur who had spent more time in an office than on a horse over the last two years. They fell at Becher's; there were no happy memories. Paul, the tall bespectacled teacher and George, the Southern drawling businessman had been picked out as the oddities amongst the jockeys. They had provided press, public and the racing folk with some good material for wry comments, especially when neither completed the first circuit.

Peccard falls at the last fence in the 1969 Kim Muir Chase at Cheltenham.

George might have appeared polite and unruffled by this rather mixed début in British racing, but underneath he was seething. He knew he had gone about it the wrong way – buying horses unseen, not having enough practice over the British fences. He sold his horses but, although retiring disappointed and dispirited, he was set upon returning to the mecca of steeplechasing. It would take a few years; there was the money to be made to finance it; there was the American title to get under his belt and there was the unhappy hurdle of a divorce from his wife.

Three years later, in the autumn of 1972, the new occupant of Ryan Price's jumping yard, Josh Gifford was woken by the telephone. The fury at having his all too short sleep interrupted was abated when an American voice drawled out that he wanted to buy a Grand National horse. Josh could not believe it, he hardly knew George and from the manner in which his horses had been sold, he had never thought to see him in England again.

Josh knew the horse he wanted, it was Ballysaggeart who was in the yard of the champion trainer from the north, Arthur Stephenson. This skilful trainer said Ballysaggeart was not for sale, but he had a great jumper who was qualified – his name was Fortune Bay, but his price was big.

George is not a conventional operator and he chose Christmas Day to drive the 250 miles north to try the horse. He liked him, bought him in partnership with his girl friend Susie Thomas and only when he raced did he find out that he had physical problems which exhausted him long before the finish. By the time he was set for the National his reputation had disintegrated and one press tipster said about him: 'If this one wins the bookmakers will be able to buy Aintree'. With his 'big' style of jumping, however, Fortune Bay gave George a great ride for a circuit; then he tired and a loose horse caused them to fall.

George in the lead in a race at the 1972 Deep Run meeting in Virginia.

All this was proving an embarrassing venture, paying so much money and not a win to his credit – just falls and being tailed off. George decided he would be better off with American horses and sent over two of his own and another couple belonging to Susie Thomas. That was when the fortunes began to swing; with 15 rides in the 1974/75 season, he had three wins.

One of these wins was on a spare ride, but very much an accidental one in the view of the trainer. Josh met George at the airport on his first of seven trips over that season to burst out rather apologetically: 'I have entered a horse in a race and it was a terrible mistake as it is an amateur chase at Huntingdon. You will have to ride it'. It was not exactly a complimentary invitation, but at least it was a ride, and despite considerable misgivings on the part of the trainer – 'God I hope he is fit', was Josh's most frequent phrase of the afternoon – George came home ahead on Soviet, to notch up his first win in a British steeplechase.

This, however, did not lead to immediate acclaim on the part of the trainer, or a host of offers to ride the horses in the Findon yard. Josh was too much of a patriot to think that American horses and riders could be better than the English. This attitude was made all too apparent in a race at Kempton. George was riding one of his American imports in a important novice chase. He came into the last fence upsides with the leaders, which included one of Josh's best novices, Top Priority. George claimed he 'saw glory coming', but he missed the glory for he landed sitting on the grass not his horse; there was no compensation from Top Priority who only came second. Later, when Josh was asked how the day had gone, George was amazed to hear 'My good horse got beaten and *the other one* fell'. George was able to make a good story out of this tactless appraisal, in the way one can about great friends. Josh Gifford and his wife the former Althea Roger-Smith had become firmly established in this category;

the better George got to know them, the more he found they generated the two essentials of friendship – fun, even when things went wrong, and respect earned by the decisions they took in all walks of life.

George himself also gained respect from people because of his enthusiasm. Only a fanatic would want to keep making that expensive 13-hours Atlantic trip, put up with the horrors of jet lag and travelling, just to ride horses over British steeplechase fences. In the beginning there were not even the wins by way of compensation, but from the 1974/75 season onwards the successes began to tot up. Three wins for that season; five for the next and by the New Year of 1977, he had in five trips accumulated six wins. This was only a few less than the leader of the Amateur table, Peter Greenall, who was making a dedicated onslaught on the title. A tilt at the championship, therefore, did seem feasible for George. He had established this great training partnership with Josh who was encouraging him, the press were hinting, the friends were urging, and George was dreaming. At Christmas 1976 the momentous decision was taken; business, home, American racing, Mastership of the hounds, everything was going to take a secondary role to winning the 1977/78 Amateur Championship.

George winning the Bi-State Cross Country Race on New Arctic.

3 The Preparation

The Trainers

The method of the enterprising is to plan with audacity, and execute with vigour :
to sketch out a map of possibilities, and then to treat them as probabilities.

BOVEE

The preparation for 'the' year had to be right. George adopted a desperate approach, that came from knowing that this was to be a once only venture. He knew that he could not give up everything a second time. This challenge *had* to be successful and he was willing to invest all his determination, time and money. To win he would have done anything, except become a teetotaller, a party pooper or lose his spirit of fun.

One of the most important factors in this championship bid were the trainers who would not only be responsible for getting his horses fit to win but had to find the animals in the first place, seek out the races that they could win and help George ride them how they ran best. Surprisingly, for a successful businessman, George made no analysis to chose these key men but ended up with them by chance of circumstance.

Ryan Price instigated the Josh Gifford/George Sloan partnership by handing over his jumping yard and the horses that occupied it to Josh. George's horses were amongst them and although soon sold, that Findon telephone number was one he knew and the easiest to ring when deciding to return in 1972.

Josh Gifford's Findon yard.

Training was the inevitable progression for Josh Gifford, the quadruple champion jockey with a record number of winners to his name. The only book he ever read was the Form book, having avoided studying by leaving home at 10 to become an apprentice to Cliff Beechenor. He rode the winner of the Chester Cup at 15 and was runner up the next year to Greville Starkey in the champion apprentice table. His prospects looked rosy until he put on two stone in one winter; this forced him to take up the slower but more dangerous sport of jumping.

Young Gifford became deputy jockey to the great Fred Winter in Ryan Price's yard and eventually achieved the remarkable feat in this secondary role of becoming at 21 years of age the Champion jockey of 1964. If Josh was regarded as the great 'jockey' of his era, the honour of being the great 'horseman' fell to his number one friend, rival and companion in a good deal of high living – Terry Biddlecombe.

Josh retired early at 29 having smashed up much of his body in racing and car crashes. He took over the Findon jumping yard when Ryan Price decided to try his hand at the the more lucrative and commercial sport of flat racing.

Josh is an honest, sensitive person, who desperately wants his horses to win; this makes training a hard life. The inevitable catastrophes of racing such as the expensive horse breaking down or the favourite failing in the big race could not always be taken in his stride; but this personal total involvement has helped to make him a top trainer.

The owners love Josh Gifford because although he is unassuming, he is enthusiastic enough to pass on a little of the fun he gets out of life whenever there is a horse or a lady around. They know, too, that the horses go well in his care because of his lifetime of knowledge, his conscience and overwhelming desire to ensure they do – and, because of the team of assistants he has built up. Number one place among these must go to his pretty wife Althea, an international showjumper, horse dealer, horsewoman, cook, assistant trainer, mother, hostess, and controller of her husband's (and George's) most wayward antics.

But Josh also has prejudices and, ironically, as George's main trainer, one of these used to be the 'amateur rider'. He has long crusaded for better opportunities for the young professionals, and against the openings for amateurs which deprived them of their rides. Josh abided by these views and although assisting George in every other possible way never gave him another owner's horse to ride. George did not deprive the lads at Findon of a single ride; in fact it had been the reverse in previous years, as his horses had provided them with rides when he was busy the other side of the Atlantic. Josh stubbornly promoted the idea that George would get much more satisfaction if he won on his own horses, but the American's win at all costs approach prevented him from being converted to that idea! His only consolation was Josh's promise that principles and plans would have to be forsaken, rides would be forthcoming, if at the end of the season it looked as if George needed rides to win the title.

George's second trainer – George Fairbairn lived at the opposite end of England to Josh, in Northumberland. This enabled George to cover the northern meetings and enjoy the warm old fashioned hospitality typical of the sporting gentry in this remote part of England.

George Fairbairn's approach to racing was business-like, rather than instinctive like Josh's. It stemmed from his first interest which was Fairbairn Chicks, a successful business, which, when sold, helped him to pursue his passion for hunting full-time. He was Master of the Tyndale, hunting their wonderful open country for 16 years, but he found himself getting more and more involved with racing. He made his name by training for his neighbour Ian Williams a horse called Rag Trade, although they sold him a year prior to his great victory in the 1976 Grand National. George Fairbairn had established himself as a trainer and this together with his business sales tactics, articulate confident manner and generous hospitality, helped him to recruit owners.

He got his introduction to George through his daughter Charlotte who went to the USA to become nanny to one of George's greatest friends, Mason Lampton. George Fairbairn having heard George Sloan was keen to get a National horse, tried to get him to buy Rag Trade. When George realized what an oppor-

An amateur race at Stratford-on-Avon.

The Hillsboro Hounds parade at the Iroquois meeting.

tunity he had missed, he was rather more receptive to the second offer made in the summer prior to going for the Championship. George Fairbairn, who had a great appreciation and an eye for a horse, picked out handsome animals. His small yard contains horses that fill the eye. They get fit along the narrow Northumberland lanes, they gallop in the fields, they learn to jump when hunting – it is an individual, informal approach to racing which helps to get the best out of some 'character' horses.

Josh Gifford with his head lad Ron James.

Josh and Althea Gifford in the winner's enclosure after Monfire's victory at Chepstow.

The Horsepower

Horsepower was the key to the Championship, and this was a sphere in which George was at a disadvantage. As a stranger, an American trying to wrest the title from the British he was not going to be offered many rides. Owners and trainers might like him, even admire him as a rider, but when it came to the pinch it was their own chaps who were going to get the rides. It was to Dick Saunders, the genial Northamptonshire farmer and one of the most talented amateur jockeys ever seen; or wiry Jim Wilson, the jockey with the strength, experience and dedication to be on par with the pros; or 26 year-old Nick Henderson, the able assistant to Britain's top trainer Fred Winter. The Etonian Henderson was well connected, with a father in the Jockey Club, relations owning racehorses and great friends that included trainer Barry Hills, who wanted to try some of his high class flat horses over hurdles. These three rivals in particular would get the rides; George had to face up to the expensive fact that it was he who was going to have to provide his own mounts.

By the winter of preparation he had accumulated a number of winners who had the potential to succeed again. The oldest were his American horses that he had imported after his disillusioning efforts at buying British. There was the tall lanky chesnut Mr Fantasy – high class allowance winner in USA belonging to Susie Thomas. He arrived in England in 1974 to win two hurdle races and two chases before his front legs started to get hot and puffy. The vets had applied their remedy of bar firing and time was given its chance. Mr Fantasy would not have seen a racetrack for over two years when George asked him to help in the Championship bid.

The second American import, Monfire, started his life in Chile. He had impressed there on the flat, and was exported to America only to run into tendon problems. George heard about him, fell for him, took the risk, and kept him in the hunting field for a season. He was a star performer and in George's book that means he could jump formidable obstacles. He flew them so easily he was entered for the spring timber races. There was no introduction via the small courses; not for the first time George headed in at the deep end. They took on the huge Maryland courses but Monfire was good enough coming third in his first ever race, My Lady's Manor. One week later in the Maryland Grand National he was lying second at the last fence when he fell. Everyone was talking

Mr Know All, winner of two chases in the pre-campaign season of 1976–77.

about him in America but George brought him to England.

That weak leg gave him some more trouble before it cleared up enough for him to win novice chases and qualify for the Grand National. Monfire was George's favourite; he loved this powerful horse who had carried him fast and safely in the hunting field, over timber and brush fences.

George sent over another whose name was appropriate to the venture – Dream and Scheme. He had been brought on especially for this year having been raced quietly on the flat in the States, earning one win and three seconds and impressing his trainer, jockey and George.

These, then, were his American partners, and the remainder were bought at British sales, off Irish farms, or from training stables. All this stocking-up depended on alert contacts, quick recognition of the right material, some wily bargaining, careful vetting, and a deal of luck.

Chance purchases at Ascot sales yielded two good winners. George went along to fill in a day between racing and ended up with Crofter who was to win hurdle races and chases for him before the horse's legs also started giving problems. He joined Mr Fantasy for a rest and bar firing and his comeback was planned for the spring of 1978.

The other Ascot purchase was Mr Know All who was one of George's most economical purchases. He came from the October sales, when George was in Czechoslavakia bruising his backside and his morale – he fell – in the celebrated Pardubice race. George returned to be told that Josh had bought this handsome big Master Owen horse relatively cheaply because of rumours about heart problems. There were never any worries about his 'heart' in terms of honesty for with his great big ears pricked he tried his level best, winning two races in 1977 and earning a third at the National Hunt Festival meeting.

The most entertaining buys were made in Ireland. In this the land of the horse, the deal is a piece of theatre. Irish wits are tuned to bargaining and it is almost more important to make it an entertaining occasion, to create a story that can be retold later than to get the best price. To take part in these deals a special jargon needs to be mastered, including such terms as 'talking in telephone numbers' – asking a very high price; 'swimmer' – a horse that with effort can be traced to English origins but has somehow got across the Irish Sea to be sold in the more lucrative Irish market; and 'luck money' – shillings or hundreds of pounds given by a successful seller to indicate his goodwill.

It was into this mysterious horse coping scene that George ventured one week after deciding to attack the title. He flew to Cork where he was met by John O'Donoghue, Josh's agent in the Republic of Ireland. This burly framed farmer and stallion specialist knew the whereabouts of any horses that were on the market. He would proudly reel off their pedigrees, their family's history, and dealing tactics to be used on the owner, but it took an alert listener because his County Cork brogue came out so quickly and softly it was almost unintelligible. John drove from farm to farm, and George heard a good deal of talking in 'telephone numbers' when owners noted his American voice. He saw some 'swimmers' but nothing that really caught his eye until they visited the farm of that daredevil follower of hounds, retired jockey Timmy Hyde. The high Irish banks of this farm enclosed small fields and large numbers of high class youngstock; but their multiplicity and expense made selection tricky. George's final choice was a four-year-old who moved on springs and had the dear advantage of a fashionable father – Master Owen.

After that purchase, there were a few more fruitless but entertaining stops at trainer's yards where the prospect had just been 'taken off the market', or was trotted out unsound to the remark 'Bee jaysees he has never been lame before', or would cost more telephone numbers. Then they headed north, but as the notorious border with Northern Ireland drew closer, John O'Donoghue's foot became increasingly reluctant to touch the accelerator. Eventually he was no longer able to withhold the reason for the slower speed. This Irish man of the world was terrified; he had not crossed that line of trouble since the deterioration in Irish circumstances. For one moment it seemed as if his fears were well founded for, soon after crossing the dreaded border, a soldier leapt out in front of the car flaring a searchlight on them and another pointed a gun through the window. Although it was the work of British soldiers it was not surprising that John went white and was unable to offer more than a few stutters in reply to the demands about his name and destination.

Allowed to move on, the atmosphere did not improve as roadside guns were trained on to passing vehicles. All was well, though, when the two travellers crossed the threshold of Josh's Northern Ireland agent Harry Ferris, a farmer/dealer, and his wife Anne, a champion point-to-point rider. George, as a Master of Foxhounds, amateur rider and friend of Josh, was eagerly offered that overwhelming Irish hospitality.

The Ferrises were determined to show off their country's most famous sport and, disregarding the problems of the crusty frosted ground, brought out the Newry Harriers at lunchtime. As George jumped those hairy banks, laughed and drank with the game Irish horsey folk, the gunmen, the soldiers, and the saboteurs seemed part of another world, not close neighbours.

None of the Ferrises' horses suited George's campaign but there were still the stock of Anne's famous father, Bill Rooney, who had been the champion point-to-point rider before his daughter. He was a trainer, stood stallions and ran a yard of hunters. All these variations of horses were crammed into equally varied accommodation. Most of the occupants were shown off to the visitors, stallions being run up, hunters and eventually chasers for George.

Arlonstown Boy, a great prospect for 1977–78 season, but he broke down after only one run.

George rode any likely prospect but it was a gangly chestnut mare that won his favour, for she had that easy long stride that made one want to ride her forever. In her second race of her career she had been well fancied (financially) by her owner. She came second, losing her owner's money and his affections for her. He was now ready to do a deal.

A price was agreed and George became the owner of the six-year-old London Light. The excitement of the deal was, however, somewhat

Castlegay makes a great leap.

diminished on his return. Josh's reaction was one of horror: 'I let you loose in Ireland and all you come back with is a mare and a chestnut one at that who has never won a race'. In time his criticism was mulled for the horse that beat that chestnut mare was Mac's Chariot, who went on to win the Lloyd's Bank Hurdle at Cheltenham.

Josh was impressed with George's other selection – the four-year-old at Tim Hyde's. This unbroken youngster who held the high hopes of so many was named Pride of Tennessee.

George left the next round of buying in Josh's hands, who picked up two Irish winners over fences, Arlonstown Boy and Castlegay. George knew they were good material after riding them at the Grand Military meeting at Sandown. Arlonstown Boy, despite giving 8 lb to the next year's Gold Cup winner Midnight Court, ran him a close second. Castlegay made brisk work of the Sandown fences until the second time round at the water, when he lost his balance on the tip of the concrete to crumple and give George a terrible fall; but he made up for it later by winning two handicap chases.

Josh made two further independent purchases. The first was an unbroken five-year-old which was out of a half sister to one of the greatest amateur rides of all time – Chris Collins's Credit Call – so he had the right type of parentage. The second was the product of another Irish trip when he found a dark brown son of Orchadist, a sire he promoted as he was the fastest horse he had ever ridden over hurdles. Orchadist's six-year-old son's name was Con Hurley and he had already won point-to-points.

The most expensive buy of all, Tiepolino, was already in Josh's yard. He belonged to a Jockey Club Senior Steward, Major Derek Wigan, who had been his elated owner during a highly successful first season over hurdles. The next season Tiepolino was comparatively disappointing and although he was fourth in the Schweppes, Major Wigan decided to replace him with a younger horse. Josh quickly telephoned George claiming 'He is bound to win four or five novice chases', and that sounded good enough to George who snapped up the offer.

That completed Josh's quorum for the start of the season, but George Fairbairn had been at work in the North collecting a few for his own yard. He already had Satanic Hymn a handsome winner of novice chases, but bought cheaply because of weak front legs. He made two additions: a small but athletic Choral Society horse called Choral Prince who was a novice over hurdles and fences and a magnificent four-year-old grey – who was out of a half-sister to the Champion Hurdle hero, Comedy of Errors – named Jubilee Sportsman.

The Jubilee Sportsmen are guests at George's home.

The Finance

Jubilee Sportsman was named in honour of his owners, a group of Americans who thought it would be fun to help George in his sporting venture. They were members of a syndicate that George put together after finding, in the spring of 1977, that he had built up his horsepower but was losing his funds. He had thought of embarking on an exploratory campaign to recruit owners for some of his purchases when his great friend, Nashville lawyer Henry Hooker, suggested a syndicate.

A basic investment of $10,000 was decided upon and for this a member would become involved in a sporting bid. With interests in eight horses, rather than outright ownership of one horse, they were likely to see some of their property running whenever they went to England, the country for which Southerners, in particular, have a great affection. Nor was it too risky an investment for a grand sale was planned at the end of the season, and, in the past, the champion amateurs Chris Collins and Peter Greenall had ended their triumphant seasons by making way above the market value of the horses that had helped them. Also, as it was a business enterprise, the American tax system meant losses incurred even in the pleasurable field of racing could be offset against other profits. The syndicate could thus be promoted as an unusual mixture of business and pleasure.

Wooing potential syndicate owners was no problem for George, who bowled over everybody with his enthusiasm for the race for the title. His friends were quick to join and the first to stump up was the instigator of the syndicate scheme, that foxhunting, shooting, tennis-playing, ladies' man Henry Hooker, who even drew in some of his friends like the Brazilian millionaire Klaus Peter, and the Texan magnate in construction and drilling footings, Jack McKinney, who had never met George. Minus one arm since an accident in his twenties, McKinney remained a great sport who hunted in his hot homelands where wolves, not foxes, were the quarry.

There was also Mason Lampton, who was George's great 'companion in fun', sharing a love of racing over fences, organizing good foxhunts, getting up to mischief, telling 'off-colour' stories and making money in business. And Mason, like Henry Hooker, brought in one of his friends, Gardner Gerrard, who was a noted man to hounds in Columbus, Georgia.

There were two who had already enjoyed owning horses that George rode in the USA, Bill Carter and Boyce Magli. Carter had tasted the fun of racing success when George won the Iroquois for him on He's Trouble, while Boyce Magli had built himself up a very successful business in real estate and was happy to invest some of the returns in the turf.

Among the unexpected takers were pretty, frail ex-ballerina Ginny Shwab, who, when she heard about the Championship bid, said 'if I have to mortgage my farm, I am going to do it'. Bruce P'Pool, who had been inveigled into hunting by his pony-mad children, thought the venture would add spice to their planned trip to the UK. Then there was Vernon Sharp, George's joint Master of the Hillsboro Hounds, who brought in his son-in-law, Ben Caldwell, an eminent gynaecologist.

Finally, there was Margaret Sloan, a lady with as mischievous a twinkle in her eyes as her son George. She was his most frequent visitor, the biggest worrier about the risks he was taking, and the most enamoured by his big adventure.

The Jubilee Sportsmen syndicate was not the only means of generating owners of horses for George. Henry Hooker himself was already the owner of Mr Know All who had won enough in George's 1976/77 campaign to more than pay his way. George's partner in his early days of British racing, Susie Thomas, who later married the architect Wayne Chatfield-Taylor, owned Mr Fantasy, Calvin Houghland, George's ex-father-in-law, who had been his major owner in all the American racing ventures, agreed to buy Arlonstown Boy soon after he ran that promising second to Midnight Court.

To these was added the versatile heir to the Campbell soup fortune George Strawbridge. His remarkable range of activities included being America's leading steeplechase owner, successful amateur rider, Master of the Andrews Bridge Foxhounds, University Professor, managing director of Tampa Bay Rowdies football team – and, not least, as a patron of George's campaign through buying that springy

George Sloan with one of his greatest supporters and owner of many of his race-rides, Calvin Houghland.

Irish four-year-old, Pride of Tennessee. Although he already had The Sundance Kid in training with Tom Jones, it had proved difficult to give George the ride on him, so Strawbridge just told his friend 'Go get yourself a horse'.

There were certainly a good number of 'sports' involved in George's race for the title; it was some support to have mustered. Although easing the situation in George's financial coffers this backing meant there was the burden of having to do well for his supporters; to live up to his sales talk of reasonable financial returns or at worst small losses, and of being able to win that Championship.

There were other people to whom George was responsible. There were his racing stables that he had built up on the farm he bought in 1968. These could not boast of all weather gallops or ultra-smart schooling fences, but there were 1,200 or more acres of beautiful

George Strawbridge and George Sloan fight it out in an amateur race.

undulating lands where horses could enjoy getting fit, galloping up steep hills popping little chicken coops, ambling down hills and taking in the frequent invigorating views. Those that needed sweetening up went hunting or were turned out. It was a relaxed atmosphere, a varied individual training system that old chasers thrived on. One, Prime Motive, was still winning at 14. It was also one of the few training stables around Nashville, so there were a good number of other peoples' horses filling a barn that, with its Southern style colonnades and stylish exterior was thought by most first-time visitors to be George's home.

Responsibility for the welfare of those valuable horses was handed over to young bearded

Brothers George and Paul school horses at Panorama Farm.

The three Masters of the Hillsboro Hounds : George, Henry Hooker and Vernon Sharpe.

Tony Sylar who had been in charge of George's horses since 1974. Responsibility for their riding went to George's lanky brother Paul who had started all this Anglo-racing bug during his year in Britain teaching at Lancing.

Then there were the Hillsboro Hounds which George had been told would be his ever since those childhood days with Mason Houghland. It finally came to pass in 1974 when his father, John Sloan retired. For two years George's enthusiasm as a young Master was directed into getting the hounds to work well – he hunted them himself half the time – and into making the hunting fun for the field. It prospered, membership rose by about 40 per cent and now he had to hand over. Henry Hooker agreed to take over the reins, sharing the work with the long respected Joint Master Vernon Sharp, who had been the first Southerner to become President of the Master of Foxhounds Association.

The greatest load of all was the business. George was going to have to take the reckless step of turning his back on a prosperous fast expanding concern. It had been his partner Seth Smith who had begun a Health Spa venture; when George joined the business in 1971 there were five of these keep fit units.

These organizations encouraged their members to use a host of mechanical gadgets, whirlpools, saunas, swimming-pools, running tracks, well-trained instructors and healthy food to get themselves fit and thin. It was an increasingly popular pastime amongst Americans who are in the throes of a 'get fit' craze, bashing flabby bodies into shape or athletic ones into more muscular versions. Consequently when George's financial acumen, skills and strength at managing a growing company and salesmanship combined with Seth Smith's quiet able judgement and technical know-how, the business boomed. In six years the numbers of spas went up nearly four times, the volume of business twenty times and the profits thirty times.

To expand a business at this rate depended on alert management, and now George wanted to throw it over and use remote controls; but George had been planning. From the moment when he had those first serious thoughts about a title bid, he had started to devise the ways and means. He had too the vital assistance of Seth Smith, his partner, who was fascinated by George's venture, understood the challenge and appreciated the significance of it all. Seth, despite having to bear the extra workload, gave him a 100 per cent support to follow his ambitions.

The field was now clear for a British onslaught but there was one problem – George could not ride. That bad fall he had off Castlegay at Sandown in March became a serious one, when a following horse had stepped directly on to his right leg breaking clean through the tibula and fibula. That meant pain,

The Hillsboro Hounds meet at George's farm in Tennessee.

One of the Cosmopolitan Spas.

hospitalization, traction, a cast all the way up the leg, crutches and depression, especially as the normal recovery time for riding from such an injury was six months. For a spell in the hospital bed and when swinging clumsily around on crutches, it seemed as if the Championship was lost, but adventurous, talented doctors and a determined patient can defy the odds.

Geoffrey Sadow had George out of the Kingston Hospital in half the predicted time, and Dr Ben Fowler, his American doctor, knew his patient and took the risks.

At the end of June Dr Fowler offered to take off the cast one month before he would do it for any other patient, as long as George was willing to accept the pain, could avoid walking on it for a whole month, and would not take a single drink. (The latter was to ensure that he was capable of remembering not to walk on it!) As for riding that was embargoed until August, though George did not tell his physician that he had already been on board in the cast. George had no hesitation in agreeing with Ben Fowler's proposition, for even with this painful risky short-cut he was going to miss a month or more of the British steeplechase season.

George was soon in better spirits despite the great pain for he could put some positive work in on his leg. He made use of his local Health Spa spending hours in the whirlpool and using the weights every day. It all helped to get the ankle unlocked and the wasted muscles revived, and by the end of July he was agile enough to take the trip to England.

Builders, trainers, friends had been warned by George that he would be there, but they thought it wishful thinking. Nobody was ready for his reappearance. The horses had only just been brought back into training, none looked fit, and most were suffering from a cough that was infecting Josh's yard.

The house on the opposite end of the Findon valley to Josh's yard that George had bought the day before he broke his leg was a shambles. Builders had reached the point when more had been demolished than constructed and there seemed no possibility of it housing anyone for months. But with George hobbling around on crutches all those behind with their work did not worry. They dismissed it as the daydreams of a harassed patient when he talked about being on the racecourse in just over a month.

Some, though took more note when he hobbled across the yard, dropped his crutches beside his most promising young horse, Dream and Scheme, and was legged up into the saddle. It was a painful process, but he could manage all but the post to the trot. That made him feel a great deal better until he returned home to America to find out his Doctor had been told of his riding antics. 'I'll kill him', was Ben Fowler's reaction and George was concerned that he would now get no further help.

He did get the assistance, though, and best of all was a plastic brace which fitted around the broken part of the leg to make riding and even posting to the trot possible and hardly painful. He was like a schoolboy beginning his holidays, and was out riding, even schooling over the fences, any horse that was possible to ride at his farm.

Just three weeks after his departure on crutches, George telephoned the sceptics in England. He was all set to go and was on his way back. The preparations were over; he was ready for 'the off'.

The aspiring champion's broken leg hinders preparations for the season.

THE SUN, Tuesday, November 18, 1975 29

THEY do it for love; they do it for money . . . but the winter game is the hardest of all. Here's the first of two super stories on the love-or-money trail.

The spotlight's on George Sloan, the flying Yank, pictured above, crashing from Monfire at Cheltenham. That was the amateur rider's reward for a 5,000-mile trip.

5,000 MILES TO FALL OFF A HORSE

By CLAUDE DUVAL

GEORGE SLOAN

A FEARSOME looking whip is the only item of hand luggage carried by the towering, six-foot American who jets across the Atlantic as often as Henry Kissinger.

He is George Sloan, the amateur jockey from the cotton picking fields of Tennessee, who has a burning yearning to win the world's greatest jump prize of the Grand National.

For Love or Money

And if ever a man was certain to get the National trip it must be Sloan — all 5,000 miles of it.

For this is the trans-Atlantic journey he makes every time he rides his horses in England, which are trained by Josh Gifford at Findon.

Special

It takes nine hours for Sloan (35) to get from his Nashville home to New York and then on to Heathrow.

The whip travels in his hand — because he is afraid of losing it!

Last season he made eight trips, but now he ... able to have breakfast in New York and then ride at Ascot in the afternoon.

"Monfire was owned by the same people who have Soothsayer. I bought him as a point-to-pointer, but he is a hell of a jumper and I would love to ride him around Aintree.

I can't believe your National will die. Hey man it's the only race known throughout the world.

The National is The Race. Not only are you taking on the other horses, but also the ..."

... see a string of horses belonging to Ryan Price and asked whether he could ride out.

"When I started training I got a phone call out of the blue from Tennessee, and George said, 'Are you going to buy me a horse to win that doggone National of yours?'

"We speak on the phone very often. He always jokes that he catches me just as I am getting up while he is just going to bed.

Jokes

PAGE 28 DAILY MIRROR, Friday, November 18, 1977

Racing Mirror — YOUR BEST BET EVERY DAY

TIEPOLINO CAN BE A GEORGE TITLE CLINCHER

By CHARLES FAWCUS

AMERICAN George Sloan is determined to become champion amateur rider in Britain this winter.

To aid his ambition, George bought Tiepolino during the summer.

Tiepolino seemed just the horse to run up a sequence of wins in novice 'chases.

And he made no mis- ... that Andy Pandy's leg injury is more serious than it seemed at first.

"Andy Pandy is a good enough horse to be patient with, and he's finished for the season," declared Fred.

This will be good news for Red Rum, since Andy Pandy was going along merrily in front until falling at Bechers second time in this year's Grand ...

...ellaman wins the Hounslow Hurdle easily at Kempton Park yesterday.

All overshadowed by Tiepolino

...ely ...ternoon at Kempton ...rday. Tiepolino's ...ichmond Novices' ... by far the most ...ormance. Ridden ... George Sloan, ...-year-old, gave an ...ay of fencing. He ... Sunrise Hill soon ...d sprinted clean ...aight to win by ...ith Heidelberg 15 ...rd.

...wner was in the ...f the stable joc...mpion, Tiepolino ...generous odds of ...loan, an Ameri...restimated rider. ... his horses, pres...tly at their fences ...t in courage, as ...en stealing the ... King four fences ... making ... later ...

... gelded. And now they are both coming good at the same time."

There are no special plans for Tiepolino, other than to win more races. Incidentally he paid a compliment to The Dealer yesterday. Tiepolino finished second to Trustful at Folkestone last time out and, on Wednesday, The Dealer had Trustful beaten when he collapsed at the third fence from home.

It was Gifford's 24th victory of the season and he is duelling for the lead with Arthur Stephenson who is blazing a successful trail in the north of England. His afternoon started in good style when Royal Judgement had no difficulty in landing the odds of 11-8 in the first division of the Vauxhall Novices' Hurdle.

Royal Judgement was enterprisingly ridden by Richard Rowe, aged 18. Apparently, Lady Rootes' gelding shows signs of temperament at home and has been ... fall over ... Sussex. ... at ... Lady ...

... his anticipated treble when Legal Branch finished unplaced behind Live Spark in the second division of the Novices' Hurdle. Similarly, Tim Forster enjoyed mixed fortunes.

Although Toy Flag experienced no difficulty in scoring at Stratford-on-Avon, Hamswell, the 6-5 favourite for the Cottage Rake Handicap Steeplechase, went lame and was pulled up aproaching the fifth fence from home. It left the way open for Brown Admiral to beat his remaining opponent, King Shaw, with some ease.

Fred Rimell said that Brown Admiral, who fell in last spring's Grand National, was operated on at the end of the season for a soft palate by Geoffrey Braine, who is the leading expert on respiratory problems in the country. If all goes well, Brown Admiral, Henry Zeisel's eight-year-old, will return to Aintree next April.

It was good to see Zellaman ... easy winner of the ... Handicap Hur... His ...

National will keep enticing Sloan back, by George!

By SUE GIBSON

THE leisurely American drawl belies the competitive spirit within. A soft Tennessee manner and a slight reticence make up the attractive exterior, but he is a young man of grit, who is determined to challenge the long-established superiority of the English jump jockey at his own game.

George Sloan wants to win the Grand National and as many other races in this present jumping season as possible; yet with 20 horses in training with English trainers, how can an American competitor be regarded as anything but an asset to English racing? But he'll steal that amateur jump title if he possibly can!

He reckons to have grown up on the back of a horse, having hunted on horseback practically all his youth in Ten...

... turned out to be very disappointing," said George.

"He was about seven or eight years old, had qualified to run in the National, and yet we never won a single race with him. In the end, he turned out to ... nal bleeding — ... perience wasn ...

The followi... decided to s... horses from T... fire was the f... point-to-points ...

"But they'r... English point... tinued George... timber fencing... The Maryland... are much m... the Grand N... you're not on... I'd rather ride... on a good ... hurdles on a b...

Six vi...

Monfire we... races, and ano... Fantasy won ... spite of leg ... there again, ... American hors... all," he said.

So he start... lish horses on... was one, who ... and was plac... Kim Muir ... behind Prolan... Eyecatcher bei...

And he foun... in Charlie ... romped home ... in a handic... who has now ... for George, ... America.

George sold ... former father-i... my best frien... that"), who wa... in an import... event back in T...

With 20 h... training ... some 10 or 12 ... cases! George ... a turn in the ... with the Giffo... top form thi... are coming mo...

His favourit... Irish import ...

... to keep horses winning races," added George.

"Monfire ...

5.0 SEPTEMBER LONG DISTANCE NOVICES' HURDLE. ... £556.80, 2nd £164.60, 3rd £74.40. Three miles.

CON HURLEY ... Mr G Sloan 1

TUDOR MYSTERY ... Tudor Treasure — ... R Goldstein 2

GRINLING GIBBONS (USA) ... P J Kelly 3

Winner bred by Mrs K O'Neill, trained by J Gifford at Findon, Sussex.

Betting: Con Hurley went from 5-4 to 7-4 before being laid and wound up at 13-8. Grinling Gibbons attracted support at 6-4 and 2-1. Ballydamus varied from 8-1 to 12-1 and back to 10-1 joining Tudor Mystery who had eased from 8-1. Precious Lord and Royal Exchange ... at 6-1, later eased to 11-1, ... in places, while Happy Snoopy ... from 10-1 to 16-1, 20-1 in a place or two.

SPORTING LIFE OFFICIAL S.P.: 13-8 CON HURLEY, 2 Grinling Gibbons, ... Ballydamus, Tudor Mystery, 11 Precious Lord, Royal Exchange, 16 Happy Snoopy, ... others. TOTE: ... Dual Forecast: £2.75.

CLOSE-UP

1 Con Hurley, ... hard-ridden and held on close home.

2 Tudor Mystery, ... seventh to three out, every chance and quicken close home.

3 Grinling Gibbons, in touch, chased leaders from three out, no extra flat.

4 Ballydamus, headway tenth, one pace from two out.

5 Happy Snoopy, ... tenth, no headway from two out.

6 Majestic Touch, well placed to tenth.

7 Wanstead Boy, close up ... weakened tenth.

8 Sophie Moon, lost touch after halfway.

Apple At Night, led to third, weakened eighth, pulled up before two out.

Precious Lord, ... pulled up before ...

Royal Exchange, ... pulled up ...

Distances: ...

12 The Sporting Life, Friday, October 7, 1977

The Captain puts Sloan on carpet

TED ALLEN at CHELTENHAM

SLIPPERY conditions put paid to the chances of several fancied runners at Cheltenham yesterday.

But it did not inconvenience Captain George, who led all the way to beat No Defence in the Notgrove Amateur Riders' Handicap Chase.

The victory landed Captain George's 38-year-old American owner-rider George Sloan before the stewards to explain the running compared with a race at Wincanton on September 30.

On that occasion Captain George was pulled up in the Newlands Handicap Chase and ... finished ... ground.

The stewards heard evidence from Terry Biddlecombe, representing trainer Josh Gifford, and also Sloan. They accepted the explanation that Captain George suffers from a soft ...

... opportunity races and amateur riders' events because he is badly handicapped and doesn't carry 12st."

Captain George was Sloan's second winner in his attempt to win the amateur riders' title and only the first two completed the course in this two and a half mile chase.

Pavement Artist looked an unlucky loser of the Lydney Novices' Chase when she slipped up on landing three out, leaving the race at the mercy of the favourite, The Bo-Weevil.

Pavement Artist, bidding for a hat-trick this season, and likely to go for the Bobby Renton Novices' Chase at Wetherby next week, was ridden by Steve Smith Eccles, who said: "The wet grass on the hard ground caused her to slide along when she had the race sewn up."

Bailey's first

... Wills Embassy Premier Chase Qualifier at Newbury is a likely objective. He is also in the Black and White Chase at Ascot."

Roman Holiday also led all the way in the Cirencester Chase and his task was made easier when his nearest rival, Gummers How, slipped up on landing at the 16th when going well.

Thirteen-year-old Roman Holiday was given to trainer Verly Bewicke during the summer by former owner Lord Chelsea.

The veteran chaser, who has ... won the Kirk and Kirk Chase at Ascot, may return to that course at the end of this month provided the ground is considered suitable.

The firm ground appeared to suit Baronial, 12-length winner of the Gotherington Novices' Hurdle (Div. I), although this four-year-old also had less to do when the favourite Roman Fantasy slipped up on landing at the last flight.

John Smith confirmed that Roman Fantasy, who had been under pressure shortly before ...

12 The Sporting Life, Thursday, September 22, 1977

American Sloan hits title trail with Con Hurley

AMERICAN George Sloan broke a leg at Sandown last season, missing a Grand National ride and the Cheltenham Festival. But now he is determined to win the amateur riders' title over jumps — a crown ...

24 THE TENNESSEAN, Tuesday, December 20, 1977

Nashville rider George Sloan takes one of his own horses, Con Hurley, over a jump on his way to a victory at Cheltenham, England, one of seven he has captured on the British steeplechase circuit.

The 'Sloan Ranger' Rides To Victory

By NICK SULLIVAN

The Sloan Ranger is riding high in England.

The Sloan Ranger, of course, is Nashvillian George Sloan, who is making a run to become the first American ever to win the coveted amateur rider's championship on the British steeplechase circuit.

SLOAN, WHO is lovingly called the Sloan Ranger by the British press, popped into Nashville this week to report that he is currently tied for the lead in the standings and is right on schedule for accomplishing his goal.

"We're having a lot of good luck right now," Sloan said yesterday. "Right at the minute I'm tied for the lead. I've ridden seven winners in 28 rides, which is 25 percent. That percentage is important, because it is right on target for what I think I'll need."

Sloan, who is backed by a group of 12 sportsmen known as the Jubilee Sportsmen, left Nashville in August to ride on the winter steeplechase circuit with the stated purpose of going down in the record books as the first American to win the amateur title. With him he took eight horses, many of them owned by Nashvillians, to ride on the circuit. Sloan has ridden the English circuit before and had won 13 races last season before he was sidelined with a broken leg.

This year, Sloan made his return ready to make his challenge "over the sticks." He is tied with Dick Saunders, England's third leading amateur last year. The tour will end in June and the rider with the most victories at that time is the amateur champion.

"IN OUR GROUP of horses that the Jubilee Sportsmen have sponsored, Tiepolino has won two important races, one at Sandown Park and another at Kempton Park," Sloan reported. "Tiepolino looks like one of the top novice steeplechasers in England this season. We're pointing him toward the Arkle Steeplechase at Cheltenham in March. The Arkle is the big novice stakes race of the year."

Sloan reported another of his horses making a big

National Hunt racetracks
Racetracks at which George Sloan won
Stables
Perth Hunt
Kelso
Ayr
GEORGE FAIRBAIRN'S
Hexham
Carlisle
Newcastle
Sedgefield
Teeside Park
Catterick
Cartmel
Wetherby
Haydock
Liverpool
Doncaster
Market Rasen
Bangor-on-Dee
Southwell
Nottingham
Uttoxeter
Fakenham
Leicester
Wolverhampton
Ludlow
MACER GIFFORD'S
Huntingdon
Warwick
Worcester
Towcester
TERRY BIDDLECOMBE'S
Stratford-on-Avon
Hereford
Cheltenham
Chepstow
LONDON
Windsor
Ascot
Kempton
Newbury
Sandown Park
Folkestone
Lingfield
TONY GRANTHAM'S
Taunton
Wincanton
Plumpton
Fontwell
FINDON
Devon and Exeter
Newton Abbot

4 The Year

August

It is not help, but obstacles, not facilities but difficulties that make men.
W. MATHEWS

After a mere six weeks' holiday, the jumpers return to divert a minute fraction of attention from their much more profitable relations, the flat racers. They return to the second-rate facilities of the holiday tracks, the baked hard ground of the rarely watered courses; but the jumping crowd are in the sport because they love it. They cannot wait to be off again, and there was one terribly frustrated amateur furiously trying to get fit in America, who thought he could be throwing his title chances away by not being amongst them.

George Sloan made it back to the home of Steeplechasing three weeks after the start of the season. On his first morning the alarm broke into his deep sleep; the clock read 6.30 am but it was 11.30 pm in Nashville, the time to which his body was tuned. Somehow he fell out of bed – he had to do it – and he would have to go on doing it six, or sometimes seven, days a week for the following 10 months. Jet lag would not act for long like lead weights on his eyes and body but there would be other reasons for making that plunge on to the carpet worse than diving into an icy pool. Lack of sleep would be a constant problem, as would the effects of driving for hundreds and hundreds of miles. Just a little too much of the stimulating beverages could possibly come into play, and an aching head or body from being jettisoned off horses would be the worst, but he knew inevitable, part of his suffering.

To ride out every morning was George's plan. It was a disciplinary regimen to ensure that his rather wayward tendencies to enjoy parties to the full – and for as long as they went on – would not interfere with his riding. It was the best means of getting very fit, and it was the only way of really getting to know his horses.

On that first morning after his return, his gaunt figure walked into the Gifford kitchen to a gibe from Josh: 'You do look rough'. The kettle was boiling, the coffees were poured, and both trainer and jockey immersed themselves in the British racing world's daily bible – the *Sporting Life*. It took a while to thaw the brain, to get the vocal cords mobilized; yesterday's winners, that day's runners were checked before attempting to speak.

Josh began to feel more alert as he settled into his morning pattern, and he told George his horses were entered up. 'D-Day' was August Bank Holiday Monday and the meeting was Huntingdon. That caused a few stirrings in

Walking before the canter work.

George's dozy head. He downed his black coffee, with very little sugar in it – he had to watch his weight – and headed towards the stables.

There were quite a few relieved faces to see that the crutches had been discarded and that the jockey of so many of the yard's horses could walk, albeit with a limp. Wisecracks flew around about that, and the slow-speaking alert-minded Ron James, who had been head lad in this yard for 15 years or more, said with a grin: 'maybe now you have got rid of your sticks you can put your own tack on'.

George made for the tack room where chalked on the board were everybody's rides for the morning. They had given him a friendly welcome putting him on the kindly Mr Know All, not one of his wayward youngsters. He went towards his old friend's box. The horse was a disappointing sight: his coat was dull and his bones prominent. Ron who had been following George, guessed reaction: 'Not too good, the old fellow's blood count was low. Don't rush him and he'll be winning you races in time'.

It was 7.30 am, there was a shout 'Let's go', and horses were led out by the lads from boxes in every corner of the yard. Ron and Josh were waiting at the corner legging up light tough lads, ambitious to prove to the 'Guvn'r' they were future champions. George came along and Ron turned to say: 'I suppose we shall have to lift him on board'. George just gave him a big wink, raised his left leg which was in good shape, and sprang easily into the saddle. 'Well you never can tell', said Ron, 'We might make a jockey of him yet'.

The horses ambled down the hill into Findon with lads adjusting their girths and stirrup lengths. They circled at the bottom so the latecomers and the Guvn'r, who was always last, could catch them up.

Then they walked on through the village of Findon to a series of 'Morning Josh', from shopkeepers and people scurrying to work. Most went on to ask 'Got any winners for us today', and Josh would give one of his frank, friendly answers that has made him such a popular resident of this racing-orientated village.

Lyn Alexander's picture of George's assistants in the race for the Championship.

Tiepolino, winner of five races during the campaign.

They trotted up the hill towards the high undulating Downs, and as they drew back to a walk, Josh came alongside George. 'Got any good ones from Tennessee?', he asked. George always had got some good ones and he spent time elaborating upon his latest story. Josh roared and trotted up to the front of the string to tell Hywel Davies, the young Welsh jockey he hoped would make good. What the story lost in not being told in a Southern drawl it gained in Josh's extraordinary take-off of that accent. Hywel was soon pealing with laughter and a few minutes later the story had been relayed once more.

Soon all the lads had had their laugh but the horses were beginning to tense up as the gallops loomed ahead. It was a sight that cleared any remaining jet lag cobwebs out of George's lungs and head. On the right, the Downs rolled down to the silent flat grey sea with the morning sunlight beams reflected in red and gold; on the left, the Downs spread away as far as the eye could see with the odd copse or house breaking the green and creamy brown of the chalky farmlands. Ahead, lay the gallops and cantering in single file up a slightly curved, gently rising all-weather gallop were 30-odd horses. Standing three-quarters of the way up was the familiar figure of Captain Ryan Price, with his trilby hat cocked on one side, and, one could imagine – for it was too far to discern – that twisted half smile on his lips. He was inspecting a far more valuable collection of thoroughbreds than he ever had in his jumping yard.

Everyone had to watch their behaviour when the Captain was in the area. One step out of line on 'his' gallops (Josh rented the use of them), and he would practice the art of which he was a master – stringing together uncomplimentary phrases, and emitting them with a roar which would have anyone who did not know the Captain quaking in the vibrations of this wrath.

The Gifford string walked on to the gallops and set off one by one to a warning 'Just steady canter now'; the lads' love of speed had to be constantly monitored. The young horses plunged and bucked, eager to be off, some of the old crafty ones felt like going home and tried to twist around towards the stables; Mr Know All just ambled into the canter showing off his good manners to the others who also settled within a stride or so. That felt better to George, the wind whistling through his hair, a powerful striding horse underneath and two great ears framing all that was before him. The hill loomed up and Mr Know All caught hold of the bit like a good horse trying to make that extra effort, but he was struggling, the energy was not there to propel him up the incline. George dropped his reins and they eased quickly into a trot.

All the horses' chests were heaving, and whiffs of misty smoke came out of their nostrils every time they let go the air of which they could not seem to get enough. Josh stood in the middle looking piercingly at just how hard those chests were pumping and trying to remember the timing of the next race each horse was scheduled to run in. 'You, Jerry, work upsides Mike; Mick with Ingrid; George, if you want to run that horse in a fortnight, don't be too hard on him, but work with Steve; the rest of you can canter steadily up Number 2.'

The string walked down the steep incline on to the rough grass between the gallops and towards where they started their first canter. Those that were working their horses pulled up their stirrups; this was the lads' chance to prove their jockeyship for they were allowed to let their mounts go, ride them out with their hands and heels for the last furlong or so of that seven-furlong gallop.

The challenges were flying around: '50p mine wins'; 'Yours Mick will only see the backside of Captain George when I let him go'; 'Not a hope with you as jockey'. The horses sensed they were in for more action as they were brought together in their work pairs. Not allowed to go forwards yet, some directed their momentum upwards with little leaps, and they snatched at their riders' arms.

Even Mr Know All leapt off – he loved this proper work. George got him to take strong hold and he kept him so close to the other horse, that the riders' feet sometimes knocked each other – that would help to stimulate Mr Know All's competitive urge. The grand horse kept going well for about five furlongs and with each squeeze from George pulled out just a little extra, but towards the end his galloping companion cruised ahead. George lacked that invigorating feeling of a strong spring underneath him ready to unleash its power.

They eased into the trot and headed directly towards Josh to circle around him, and allow his quick eye to inspect the flanks and nostrils, to see how they were breathing. 'Not so good, eh George', said the trainer. 'Needs time'.

The procession ambled back down the stony track, stopping to give the horses a mouthful of grass before returning to the yard. The stable was short staffed, which usually happens at the beginning of the season with the flat yards still in full swing. George sponged off his own horse, put him away and then limped into breakfast.

The bacon and eggs smelt delicious and the Guvn'r's pretty blond missus's face broke into a broad smile upon seeing that their Amateur Championship candidate could actually walk under his own steam. She made solicitous inquiries about how his leg stood up to the work, and a cheeky remark about the handicap the leg would be on the dance floor. George felt happy that the Giffords were going to be part of his life for the next 10 months.

Over breakfast, it was racing and more racing. The *Sporting Life* got its second, and more thorough, run through, occasional comments were passed and one horrified shout came from George upon reading that the amateur John Sharp had won his second race on Esoteric. 'I have just got to get going Josh', said George. That made Josh realize he had an extra training

Back to the yard.

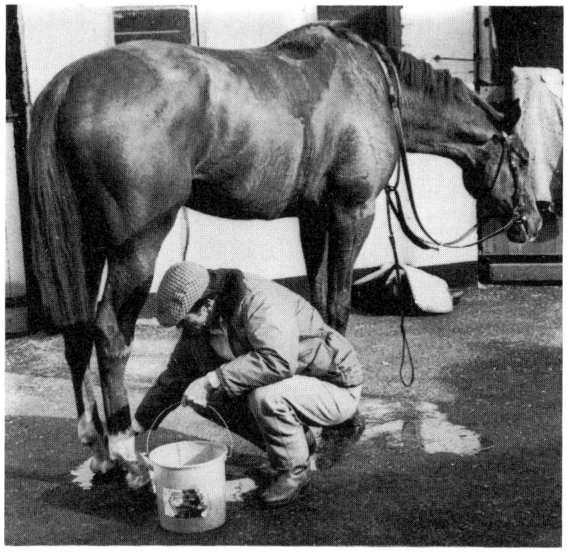

George cleans off his horse.

A breakfast with Josh, Bob Champion, George and (standing) Broderick Munro Wilson.

The essential man in the yard, the blacksmith.

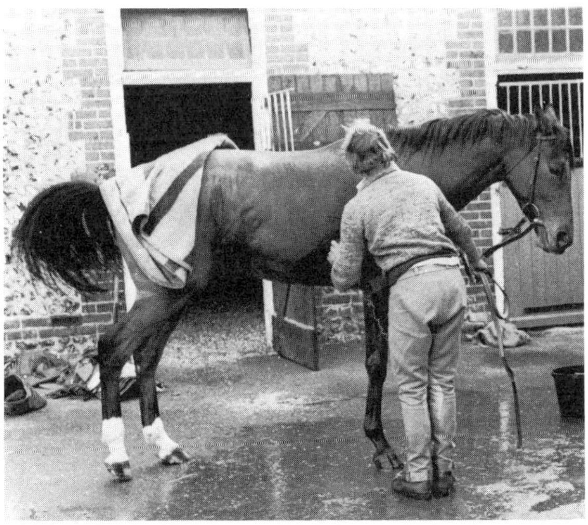

Washing down the Findon yard's star, Kybo.

problem for the season – keeping his over-anxious, over-eager Amateur Title chaser from rushing the horses to the races.

The telephone was going all the time, owners wanting to know when their horse would run, how their horse was, whether they could get a lift with Josh. Breakfast was far from a peaceful interval between 'lots'.

Now it was 9.45 am, and the jockeys were legged up again; this time, George was on his American four-year-old import Dream and Scheme. He was a beauty and he extended up the gallop to give George that exciting elation of being on a good one.

After putting away his 'special' it was into the office to give Josh's long-standing secretary Judy Bradley an extra work burden. George wanted to be involved in the entering and his major concern was to enter wherever and whenever it was possible. He was determined that he would never have cause to regret that an effort to save a few pounds in entry fees cost him the Championship. Hence the *Racing Calendar*, the weekly publication containing all the following week's entries had from September onwards, horses 'owned by G. Sloan, trained by J. Gifford', filling the pages. They were entered at obscure courses in every corner of the UK, all in the hope that one of these smaller meetings might stage a race that no one else thought of entering and was less difficult to win. This policy cost George a great deal of entry money. It meant that his horses travelled more than any others in the yard to run in the easier races at far away tracks; but this was a do or die effort to win that Championship.

The entries settled, Josh and George walked up to the gallops to tread in the divots and check the fences that had been schooled over that morning. Then it was back to the office for more of that endless telephoning which punctuates a trainer's life – press wanting to get stories; owners to know about their horses; and calls to clerks of courses to find out about the going and other trainers to discuss where they were running their horses. A little after one o'clock, Josh and George hurried out doors for the first real break of the day. They were off to 'church' – not literally but it worried Josh and George if they kept on saying 'just off to the local', so they gave it the code name 'church'. Actually drinking was not the main purpose of these frequent visits. For hours on end George winged bits of metal at the dart board for he had determined that mastering the art of dart playing was secondary only to winning the Championship. George wanted to return home to Nashville able to play one game better than his friend Henry Hooker.

After 'church', it was time to catch up on some of that sleep lost between Nashville and Findon, and to dream. To dream about Huntingdon in ten days' time. He knew the horses were not fit because Josh had been expecting a much later start from his invalid jockey. He too was hardly fit enough, and what about his nerve – would he have lost his reckless 'it's not me that will ever fall approach'? Every time he thought of the traction, the crutches, the pain and the depression, he knew that he wanted to avoid doing *anything* that would make him go through that again.

But he had to go to Huntingdon. The meeting was on a Bank Holiday; there were four others that day, dispersing the opposition, and anyway none would be too high class as good horses were preserved for the softer going and the feature races in midwinter. The races at Huntingdon would be much easier to win than those later in the season.

There was another explanation for starting at Huntingdon. He had to put on a show for those who had supported him. Two of the syndicate couples Henry and Alice Hooker, and Texans Jack and Claudine McKinney were in England. They had come to see the man who was going to earn them money, fun and glory, start his campaign.

Bank Holiday Monday was a rare day when the English sun was showing off that it could be the equal of its Mediterranean counterpart. With no sea nearby it was just the day to go racing, and thousands made their way to the flat, utilitarian course at Huntingdon. They included a good number of George's wellwishers for this was Gifford home country. Josh's mother and brother Macer – himself a past Amateur Champion – lived close to the course. George had stayed and been to parties with them many times; getting himself talked about by swinging from the hotel's chandeliers on Christmas Day, getting himself liked by the men after telling a few off-colour stories, and loved by the girls when he directed the odd wink, etc, in their direction.

Some of the Sloan supporters made their way to the saddling-up boxes to see his horse Castlegay prepared for the third race. It was a routine procedure, but there was none of the monotony of a routine to anyone involved with that horse; Castlegay himself was quivering as he was backed into the narrow stall. He knew about the excitements and strains that lay ahead.

Snowy, the ageless travelling head lad stood one side, and Josh on the other. They murmured instructions to each other as the chamois, weight cloth, number cloth, saddle and surcingle were put on. Snowy had done this millions of times, having started in French racing stables in 1926. This great experience made him even more meticulous – he knew there could be no short-cuts, there was too much at stake.

As Castlegay was led off to the paddock, Josh laughed, joked and explained the racing to the syndicate owners. His job now was to make them enjoy it, he could do no more for the horse. They walked into the centre of the paddock with the entrants for this two-mile handicap chase encircling them. Conversation went in fits and starts for pre-race nerves were getting the better of everyone. No one talked about it but everyone was thinking: 'what if he falls?'; 'is the horse fit?'; 'what about the rider?'; 'will it hurt him to run?'; 'is he good enough?'; 'could he win?'; 'is it worth a bet?'.

Then into the paddock came the jockeys, a bobbing mass of bright silk colours, but one stood out and drew comments for he was walking with a terrible limp – could he really ride in a race?

A steward called George Sloan aside. 'Have you ridden in a race since your accident?'

'No'. George was worried this could be bad trouble.

'Have you passed the Doctor as fit?'

George had his questionable defence ready. 'I ride on an American licence, as a visiting rider I do not have to.'

There was a long silence while the steward weighed up whether he should report the matter – the sun, the look on George's face had their effect. 'Go get on your horse'.

Josh legged him up and led him around the paddock out on to the course all the while giving instructions. 'Give him an easy race, he's not too fit and has a lot of weight. He takes a good hold but keep him back if you can. Tuck him in behind the others so he cannot pull his way to the front – have a good ride.' He snapped off the lead rein and George was on his own – back on the racecourse, ironically on the same horse who had done all the damage just six months before at the Sandown water jump.

The first meeting of George's season at Huntingdon. George goes out watched by travelling head lad 'Snowy' Davis and Althea Gifford.

From the moment the flag went down they galloped at a great rate. The hard going and the flat 11-furlong circuit meant it was no test of stamina. The jockeys did not have to contain their horses to preserve their energy, speed was all important. George had no trouble in holding Castlegay up, at the rate they were going it was his maxium speed. They flew the fences, over the water – that was psychologically a good one to put behind them – up over the open ditch in front of the stands. He kept on the inner, close to the rails – less far to go – but a horse banged him. George's injured leg hit the rails with a crack – the pain was excruciating – 'Shit, I have busted it again', were the jockey's rueful thoughts.

A few yards further and Castlegay stopped pulling; from having been a handful, suddenly power whooshed away like a popped balloon – Castlegay's lungs could no longer get enough air to keep going – he had blown up. There was little point in battling on and although better for the morale to finish, it could damage his and his horse's legs. They returned to the paddock to be greeted by supporters attemping to minimize the pain of this ignomonious end: 'horse was not fit'; 'he needed the race'. But there was reassurance, at least, in that George's leg was in one piece – he could still stand on it.

There was another ride later in the afternoon and George knew he was good enough to win. It was on his little American import Dream and Scheme who had trounced one of Josh's best novice hurdlers, Green Fingered, when working on a racecourse four days before. The bookies were given fistfuls of notes by Americans for Dream and Scheme, and Josh was known to produce 'good 'uns', so despite this being his first run over fences the starting price tumbled. He started the second favourite for the two-mile novice hurdle.

Dream and Scheme was running well and was up with the leaders until they made the right-hand turn towards the finish. George heard a roaring noise, his horse, on which he was so 'high', was choking and could not go on. It was a momentary problem, he caught his breath and was soon pulling again eager to catch the others; but it was too late they were past the winning post.

George had not been expecting too much with the horses being relatively unfit; but to have to pull up them both, that was a severe blow. Morale, however, was raised a little when syndicate owner Claudine McKinney said 'If you are disappointed for us don't be – we are just having a ball'; but was quickly crushed again when husband Jack drawled more seriously 'Well, I am disappointed – if you don't win the first, you can't win them all'.

George working up the all-weather gallop.

September

The roar of the race-course died behind them,
In front were their Fates, they rode to find them,
With the wills of men, with the strength of horses,
They dared the minute with all their forces.

JOHN MASEFIELD

September is usually a warm month, and, with the ground still resembling iron, trainers keep their good horses at home. There are plenty of those 'easy' races to be won, all that is needed is a horse that will gallop on the hard and an owner and trainer that thinks it worth the risk to let him do so.

George was willing to take any risks to help him win the Championship, but two days after Huntingdon he was given one opportunity that even he had second thoughts about.

After midday diversionary activities bidding for furniture at a Worthing auction sales, George returned to the Giffords for tea. Josh could not wait to tell him: 'I have a gift for you. There are only two horses in your race tomorrow and the other one is Frodo which is not much good'. George's heart rose and sank pretty quickly. He was reminded of his maxim 'luck is when preparation meets opportunity', for he knew they had not the preparation to meet the opportunity.

Mr Know All was the horse. He was not in good enough condition to win and was only running because his owner Henry Hooker was in the UK. Now George would have to be hard on him making him gallop faster than was good for him. He would have to do this because of the punters' money – Mr Know All was sure to be the hot favourite – because of the stewards who would ask for explanations if he did not appear to be trying; and because there was a chance with such poor opposition that he could get his first direly needed win in the Championship race. Poor Mr Know All.

This badly timed 'gift race' was to be held at Fontwell, the closest track to the Findon stables and one of the most popular in Southern England. Freshly painted, rather quaint grandstands look out on a figure of eight steeplechase track. There is an intimate atmosphere with crowds gathering in the centre, to get within a few feet of the horses as they hurtle over the fences.

It is a tricky track to ride, though, for being a figure of eight, nearly every fence is on a turn: with the small circuits jockeys have sometimes found the counting too much for them. The last time George rode there he reached the winning post way ahead of the field, came back to the trot to wait for the cheers appropriate to his easy victory. All he heard were shouts and the thunder of hooves as the horses galloped on by. His poor horse Monfire was booted on again by the red faced American jockey, but despite this embarrassing 'breather' they still managed to get past the winning post first. There were a few cheers but mostly laughter and teasing.

George was sure of the number of circuits this time but Mr Know All was short of the energy needed to come off the turn, to take the bit and pull on into those 4 ft 6 in birch fences. Instead in Fontwell's feature race of the afternoon he steadied into them, and without the momentum, climbed over, his head high in the air. To spectators it looked as if he had an appalling jockey unable or unwilling to push him on. Only the trainer, the lads and the jockey himself knew that the energy was not there, that when George pushed nothing happened. Mr Know All trailed in behind Frodo and the murmurs on the course were that this American who was going for the title could no longer ride, had lost his nerve after breaking his leg. The punters who had laid their money on his horse were quick to direct their disappointment at him, the odd one even booed; they were bitter, but so was George – a horse can certainly make a fool as well as a hero out of a man.

When, after these upsets at Huntingdon and Fontwell, he was beaten two lengths by Fred Rimell's heavily fancied Evening Air a couple of days later, it was almost as exhilirating as a win. George was reassured that if his horses were fit enough, he could give them a good ride; this time his six-year-old, Con Hurley, jumped fluently round the hurdles of Stratford's even track on the edge of the River Avon.

Con Hurley would win a race for him – George was sure of that – but of the others Dream and Scheme had come back with tired, puffy legs after Huntingdon, Castlegay was being victimized by the handicappers and seemed unlikely to win a race with the weight he had to heave around, and Mr Know All was not right. George became panicky – he had to have more horses, he could not let the year slip by – he had to go on another buying spree. Josh found him out of his yard the eight-year-old Captain George, who had already won that season and usually managed three or four victories when the ground was hard. But there did not appear to be any others on the market so it was off again to the birthplace of the best steeplechasers, Ireland.

The two Gifford contacts had been alerted as to George's desperate need for horses so they both arrived at the airport to meet their horse-coping visitors. They set off in a convoy of two cars, Harry Ferris with George and John O'Donoghue driving Josh. They sped along deserted Irish roads, hardly passing a car, but when John O'Donoghue stopped to ask a local bicyclist directions, Harry was not prepared for such a disturbance to their uneventful drive. The only two cars in the vicinity bumped straight into one another.

That woke everyone up but they were really wide awake when they saw the horse that was the object of their visit. He was a handsome 16.1 hands high chestnut who looked good and felt even better when George rode him. Josh and George were very keen, but the owner Mr Henley was not around. The lad in charge just said: 'You can buy the horse if you can find the man. If he is not at the greyhound stadium then he could be anywhere'. Well he was not with the greyhounds as he was in Cork Hospital.

Told of this unfortunate address, the whole entourage – Josh, George, Harry and John – traipsed into the poor invalid's room. Josh adopted dealing tactics which could not have enhanced the patient's well-being, joking 'As you're not going to live much longer you might as well sell the horse'. The tactics resulted in a deal, but the owner was in such a state that he discharged himself from the hospital. Nobody knows whether it was to defy Josh's prognostication, or to look after the horse who was going to earn him money.

Everyone was in high spirits about that deal over the horse, which was named Super Travel, and just in the right mood to go on buying. Their next candidate turned out to be a sway back horse but he moved beautifully. They thought it worth the risk, especially as he was bound to be cheap. The Irish farmer, however, was very hesitant to even put him on price but as Josh kept badgering he eventually named a figure the size of which had Josh reeling. John and Harry hurried away from the scene, calling to Josh to follow. Reluctantly he got into the car which was about to move off when the farmer appeared at the window. That was good tactics, walking away, thought Josh as the farmer asked what price he would be willing to pay. Josh opened his mouth to name a figure but all that came out was an 'ouch' for he was punched in the ribs by John, who hissed as he drove off: 'Never educate a mug, especially one without a handle!'

John planned to return to do a deal when the over eager Findon buyers who lacked the Irish guile were on their way back home. He did return, but he had to admit even he could not educate that mug. The horse was never bought.

George had to return to the USA after their Irish trip to testify before a Federal Trade Commission on Health Spas. Josh was a trifle relieved to be rid of his over anxious owner/jockey and to have time to get the horses in better condition. But George spent only 10 days in America; he was eager to get back to spur on his trainer, to get himself fitter and to be ready if any easy race came up.

Castlegay was one horse they were going to have to run a few times with no prospects of winning. He had won a race in the spring impressing the handicappers so much that they gave him enormous weights to carry. Josh knew that Castlegay was not good enough to carry the burden and his only option was to 'run him down the handicap' to race him, and prove that the handicappers had overestimated his ability. So it was away on the 150–odd miles to Taunton to give 29 lb to the winner, to come third and to discover later the price to be paid. The hard ground, the heavy weight and the lack of condition all added up to strain Castlegay's front legs. He now joined Dream and Scheme on the third lot at Findon; no hard canters, just easy exercise and constant treatment on those tired legs.

Next stop after Taunton was a return to the course at Shakespeare's home town of Stratford-upon-Avon. It was an easy race and the plan was to try out Mr Know All – but he was not ready to be tried out. Once again he made George look like a second-rate amateur and they trailed in last.

The horses were just not in form but his two-bedroomed cottage – bought because of its magnificent view of the Findon valley and the gallops beyond – was at last fit for him to move in. At least the builders had put in the windows and blocked up gaps in the outside walls which made it just possible to camp in. Taking advice about the dangers of damp in an unused bed, George borrowed an electric blanket from the Giffords to warm up his sleeping area.

George went to sleep content that at last one part of his plan for the year was functioning – his house – but he woke up to ominous smells that it might not be functioning too safely. Smoke was billowing from the second-hand bed he had had bought at an auction, and his first-hand expensive Down Continental quilt. Instant aquatic action was taken to quell the problem but then it started to stink.

Surely nothing else could go wrong, luck could help him a little bit, especially as that afternoon he was due to run at his favourite track – National Hunt's premier course at Cheltenham. The track is situated on the edge of this spa town against a magnificent backcloth of the Cotswold hills. The course is long, undulating and very testing, for the beautifully built tough fences have to be jumped on uphill slopes, down unbalancing inclines, and to finish, the horse has to take on a steep rise to the

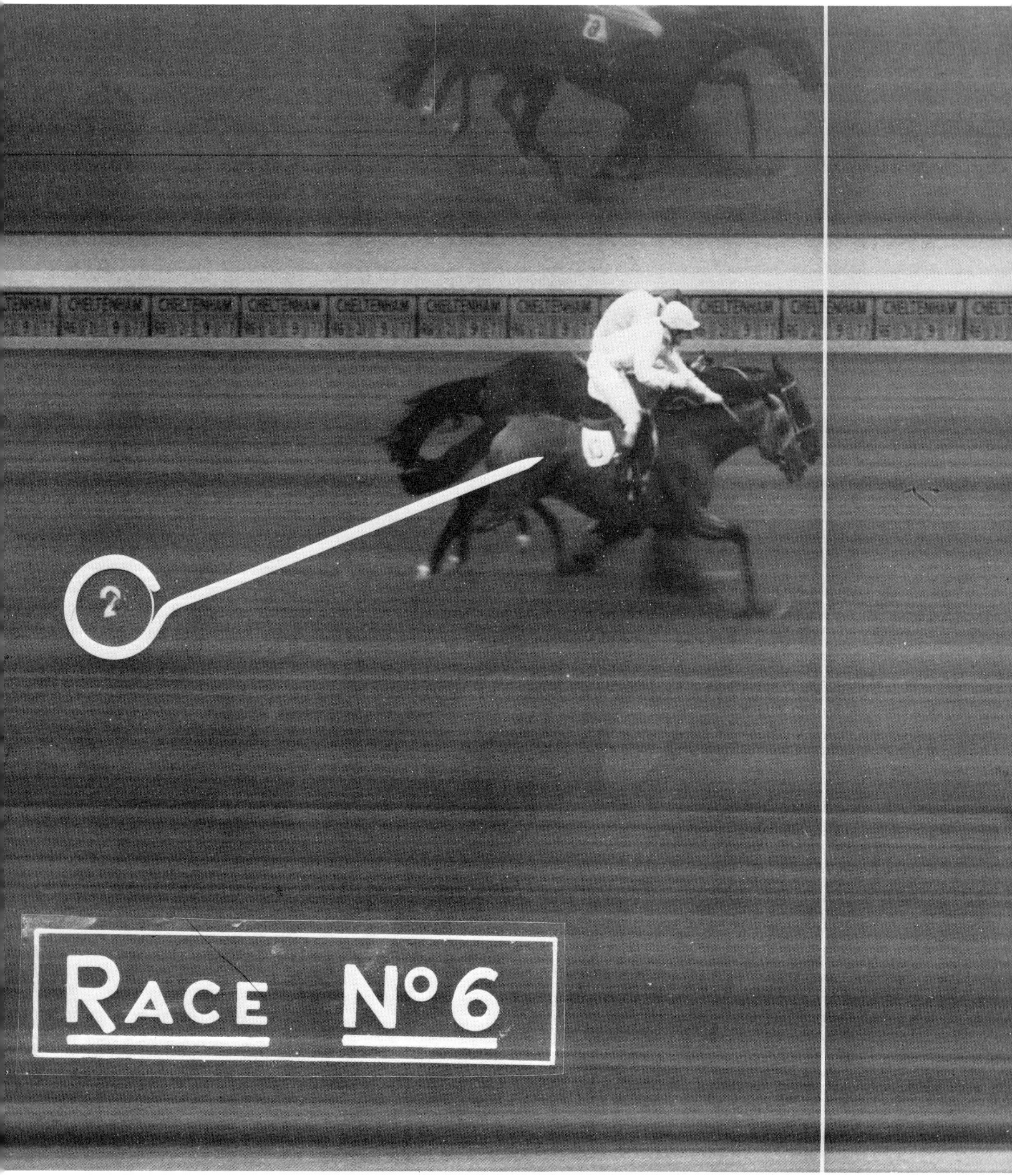
CHELTENHAM
2
RACE No 6

post up which only the bravest and toughest can gallop.

George had that tough horse to ride as he was on his Stratford second, Con Hurley. They were in the long distance three-mile novice hurdle and started favourites after their previous impressive run. All went well, until, landing over the last hurdle, George heard the steps of a horse getting closer and closer. He was in front, but he knew Con Hurley had no powers of acceleration, and ahead lay that long steep hill to the finish. George kept kicking, urging and swinging his stick. Con Hurley kept running but that horse was getting nearer and nearer. At the post George thought he had lost – yet another failure. But as Josh came to meet him, to lead him into the most coveted winners enclosure in the world of National Hunt, over the Public Address came: 'First – Number 3'. He had done it; he had his first winner of the season; and he had the super exhilaration of having succeeded in a great tussle to the finishing line.

It was the closest race of George's life and the photograph later proved it, for the only part of Con Hurley that was in front of rival, Tudor Mystery, was the vital part – the nose. One nod of the head later, and he would have been beaten; George would have been despondent, instead he was celebrating. With only winners counting there is a very fine dividing line indeed between elation and despondency in the race for the championship.

The first winner of the season – Con Hurley being led into the winner's enclosure at Cheltenham.

The official photograph: Con Hurley wins by a nose at Cheltenham.

October

Effort is only effort when it begins to hurt.

GASSET

October lies in no man's land. Just as the weather can be part of summer or winter, the best racing can be National Hunt or Flat Racing. The National Hunt activities however, are on the upswing, and although there are no major races the jumping stage expands from the country courses to include, for the first time, the major London tracks.

In the October of George's year there was hardly any rain, and he had to rely on the few horses who liked galloping on ground that jarred them as much as the main road. The horse with the best record in these conditions was his September purchase, Captain George. George's début on him, however, had been calamitous. In a two-mile handicap at the galloping West Country track of Wincanton Captain George could not keep up with the field, jumped badly and was eventually pulled up by his forlorn new owner.

Just three days later, during a breakfast planning session, Josh said Captain George should run in a race at Cheltenham. George was taken aback as one of the Cheltenham runners was No Defence, a horse that had trounced them in that disappointing Wincanton race. Therefore this was surely illogical – poor placing – but Josh was insistent: 'It's a different course and there is only one horse to beat. You have got to take your chance'.

Josh was unable to back up his confident prediction with his support; he could not go to the meeting and asked his old friend and rival in Champion Jockey, Terry Biddlecombe, to act as substitute trainer at the races. This immensely popular, grinning ex-champ, now ran a breaking yard, was a radio and television tipster and commentator; but he enjoyed 'playing trainers', an occupation he so nearly took up. He saddled Captain George and tried to give a good owner 'chat up' to George's mother who had come over for 10 days. It must have been difficult, though, for nobody could understand why Captain George had been sent on the 300 mile round trip from Findon to run against a horse that had soundly beaten him five days before.

Well, Captain George set off in front, and to everyone's amazement, and some punter's anger, he stayed there. It was huge grins from the Sloan contingent for there is nothing like getting an unexpected winner, especially at Cheltenham. But there was a good deal of teasing too, and David Nicholson the trainer of the hot favourite, No Defence, came over and felt George's forearm muscles: 'What have you been up to my boy?' Although George had not been pulling his horse that day at Wincanton, and this was no massive betting coup, he was obliged to explain matters to the stewards. The excitement of this startling victory was duly interrupted by the announcement: 'Stewards' Inquiry. Please retain your betting slips'.

George, with Josh's 'stand in' in the West Country, Terry Biddlecombe, had to go and make their explanations to a group of eminent figures on the Turf. Terry was none too happy that his 'stand in' role should have led him into such a predicament, and murmured to George: 'The bastards – my having to call them "Sir" and I shall be shooting with most of them on Monday!'

George also found it difficult to follow Britain's respectful customs but he had learnt a lesson two years before. On his first encounter with the stewards he saw a chair, sat down on it to which there was a rather frosty reaction from one of the distinguished gentlemen of the Turf: 'Would you mind standing up?'. George remained standing this time to make his unusual explanation of the difference in Captain George's running. 'I really cannot explain the difference. I had just bought the horse when it ran at Wincanton, he started choking and I wondered what sort of horse I had been palmed off with. Today he had everything his way, he ran beautifully and never choked.' It was too naive an account to be anything but honest and the stewards dismissed them without a reprimand.

That win started October off on a note of optimism, but racing rarely keeps its participants elated for long. Dream and Scheme, the horse George had the greatest hopes for, choked again during his second run at Uttoxeter. That meant he needed a soft palate operation, and a rest from racing.

After Uttoxeter, George drove north for his first ride from his second stables. Trainer George Fairbairn was full of optimism, claiming Choral Prince was ready to win. But at the elegant and stylish Ayr racecourse, they trailed in last in the novice hurdles. Choral Prince appeared to be yet another useless assistant in George's Championship trail.

George returned South to try out his favourite ride, Monfire, in a valuable Saturday race, the Charisma Tapes Chase at Kempton. Monfire jumped magnificently and finished an impressive third. George was delighted, but not for long; Monfire's legs suffered on that hard ground, a suspensory was strained and he had to be sidelined for the rest of the season.

The day of that Kempton race had started badly at Findon. It had rained the night before, softening the ground and making it feasible to school the most expensive member of George's string, Tiepolino, over fences. After a canter, Josh and George rode over to the fences where a mist enveloped the black masses of birch so that they loomed up suddenly out of the whirling grey moisture. They were not ideal conditions, nor was there a horse available to jump alongsides Tiepolino; but Josh was not worried for the horse had schooled brilliantly in the spring over those big fences. George cantered casually down to the first fence, which Tiepolino skimmed over. The next fence was being rebuilt so they skirted around it and came a little crooked into the big open ditch. Tiepolino was startled, slowed up and then leapt so high in the air that it was difficult to know who was more upset, the jockey, who thought he was going to be jumped off, or the horse for having to put in such a massive effort to clear the fence.

It turned out to be the horse for when they approached the ditch the next time, Tiepolino proved his athleticism by stopping so quickly that only George himself jumped the fence.

Josh's laughter at the fiasco of the first jump turned to anxiety and he roared at his 'amateur' to pull himself together, to strip off his coat and to get down to work; but the results were still

Monfire (right) *jumps alongside Graigue House and Zarawyn at Chepstow.*

6

poor. Tiepolino only scraped over those fences. Breakfast was gloomy that morning – nobody said it, but everybody felt it: had they through this casual approach ruined a good horse?

The professional jockey to the stable, Bob Champion, was called in. He was a master at schooling horses having learnt to ride, not on the gallops but at the best school for horsemen, in the hunting field. His family had been professional huntsmen for three generations. Bob was warned about Tiepolino's nasty habits and took suitable precautions to rouse him as they approached the open ditch. But like George it was only Bob who jumped the fence, Tiepolino remained firmly on the take-off side.

Josh's face clouded, and he released some of his worry in a few hot words to his stable jockey. That made Bob build up an extra store of determination; this was enough to get Tiepolino over the fences, but they only just made it. Josh knew the horse had jumping ability and he decided the adrenalin generated on the racecourse might help him to produce it. In the company of other horses Tiepolino might be encouraged to jump more fluently, so after one more disappointing schooling session he was sent racing.

Josh's stable jockey Bob Champion and George walk out to the parade ring.

Josh gives directions during a schooling session.

Jane Sloan (née Thorne) riding Spartan Missile at Cheltenham.

George jumping the water on Sir Tacks.

George riding for home and victory at Newton Abbot on Helpex.

Mrs Sloan leads in Crofter after his victory on the final day of the season.

Huntingdon with its straightforward galloping track was chosen for his début over the big fences. With his history as a top-class hurdler he started hot favourite. He galloped on into the first fence and jumped it brilliantly; that made George feel quite confident. Then three horses fell in front, it left Tiepolino and the renowned reluctant jumper Big Ribot in the lead. This was the contest; the two horses vied with each other as to who could go slowest into these 4 ft 6 in birch hedges. They tried to stop and were only kept going by frantic efforts from their two unhappy jockeys – George and Jeff King, one of Britain's strongest riders. For a spectator who had no money invested it made a funny sight, but George, who was hoping Tiepolino would be the cornerstone in the race for the title, had a miserable ride, ending up in fourth place.

The day became even unhappier when Captain George gave him a fall in the next race, and Castlegay had to be withdrawn because the ground was too firm for his suspect tendons.

The next day brought compensations, but not in the Championship race. The latest British equestrian craze was Cross-Country Racing in which teams of four or five dashing contestants raced over a semi-prepared cross-country course. People loved to watch it – there was always a high accident rate; sponsors queued up to give high prize money with Princess Anne and the Prince of Wales being regular competitors, and the numbers of competitors continued to grow, thanks to the fun of the team atmosphere, the stimulation of dashing across country and lack of demands for specialist skills.

'The Racing Amateurs' – George, Jim Wilson, Nick Henderson and Dick Saunders.

New Arctic jumping a drop fence in the Grafton Cross-Country Race.

George joined the 'Amateur Riders', a team made up, ironically enough, of the main contenders for the amateur steeplechase title. On weekdays they drove all over the country to get rides and try in every possible way to beat each other on the racecourse, but on Sundays they got together to try and beat the other teams. It was a good boost for British – and American – sportsmanship.

On the Sunday following that dismal Huntingdon race day, the Amateur Riders did beat all their rivals. George was given something more than money to help compensate for his racing failures. First prize included a night out with the bunny girls at London's Playboy Club.

Josh did not take on the training for these amateurish sporting 'races', giving the job to his younger brother, Macer, who had been forced to retire as a jockey after severe concussion. He now ran a 700-acre farm close to Huntingdon where he looked after George's Cross-Country racehorse, New Arctic, who had won under National Hunt Rules a year before, but only because every other horse in the race fell. His great asset was his jumping and George brought him over from America especially to run in the most frightening race in the world – the Pardubice Steeplechase in Czechoslavakia. New Arctic disgraced himself by falling at the easiest fence on the course, but his performances in the British Cross-Country races convinced George that he had to try again; but only after the title race was over.

As October drew to a close, it seemed that success in a future Grand Pardubice was more likely than his Championship bid. Three of his horses were already out of action. His new horse, Super Travel, was not going to be fit to race for a long time, as a rough journey and six days stabled on the dockside had made him very weak and resulted in a bad cough. George had only two wins to his credit and his percentage of winner to rides – 11 per cent was abysmally low.

But, George had to go home. The business needed a check over and it was the opening meet of the Hillsboro Hounds. His return was appropriately timed to coincide with the most important hunting occasion of the year.

Some of the winner's spoils in the Playboy Cross Country Championship.

November

Where the storm-clouds gather, where the strong
winds stride
Autumn calls to England and bids her bravest ride
OGILVIE

Riding out in the winter.

In November, the complexion of National Hunt steeplechasing changes. It is colder, the frosts start, the trees look bleaker as their leaves fall away, but the racing gets better and better. Each week increasingly important races are staged, the good and great horses make their seasonal débuts, and every stable begins to find out whether the horses that looked so promising at home can hold their own on the racecourse.

George could not let one of the best months in the National Hunt year slip by – he was back from Tennessee in less than a week. Now he had to put on a good show; his parents were coming over. They wanted to see for themselves why

British racing kept luring their son across the Atlantic.

The 73 year-old Mr Sloan decided to savour all possible angles – even riding out. On his very first morning he was legged up on to Castlegay who did not prove responsible towards his illustrious cargo. When up on the Downs he gave a few bucks, depositing Mr Sloan on the grass. Josh came cantering up, checked all was well and said: 'The lads will be pleased that's some more money for the kitty'.

The kitty is the collection for the lads' Christmas Party and all those who commit misdemeanours – getting run away with, falling off, etc, have to contribute. Thanks to George's friends the kitty was growing fast. The constant stream of Americans that arrived to support him were usually persuaded to get into the swing of things by riding out. Some survived but quite a number tasted the top gear of his horses to disappear over the horizon out of control; others got removed from the saddle 'to buy a bit of the Downs', but even George made his contributions including being bucked off Castlegay, and that was some reassurance to his father.

After this sore start to the trip, the Sloans made their way to Fontwell to watch George try out Mr Know All again. George was none too happy about the prosepct as it was on this local twisting track that Mr Know All had run so badly. But two months of good food, and special blood treatment had restored him as a racehorse. He swung on into the fences, made George look like a champion rider, and galloped past the post an easy winner.

Mr Know All was back in form so Josh wanted to make good use of his high spirits. Just four days later he was loaded into the box for a 400-mile round trip to the little Norfolk track of Fakenham. It was a country course lying in the midst of the flat Norfolk marshes, where it neither attracts big crowds or large numbers of runners. It was worth the journey for Mr Know All's race was an 'easy' one, the main opposition

Mr Know All being led in by his lad Gary Lucas after a win at Fontwell.

being the leading rider in the Amateur table, Dick Saunders on Yellow Stone. George and Mr Know All overtook them one fence from home and quickened to win their second race in five days.

Now George was only one win behind Dick Saunders in the Championship table. Spirits were high and Mrs Sloan was acclaimed as George's lucky mascot after leading in three of his four winners; but her biggest test of bringing luck was still to come; George was going to try out Tiepolino again.

Josh astonished George by announcing that Kempton would be the venue. This was one of England's premier tracks, the fences were big, if a little softer than they used to be, and the class of horse running was always high. As George's main concern for the winter was to win races, and, as his last performance on Tiepolino had been so dismal, it seemed sensible to be less ambitious. But Josh knew his horses, Kempton is a flat, fast track which gives horses a chance to run; it would suit a real racehorse and that was what he thought Tiepolino to be.

George was sceptical and very anxious. Tiepolino had had a race with Bob Champion in the saddle and had jumped well enough to come second. If George could not get him to run it did not speak too much for his riding and also meant that he had persuaded the syndicate to make an expensive 'dud' investment for his Championship bid.

George walked into the paddock to find he had some new supporters in this nerve-wracking race. George Strawbridge had flown in for a meeting to recruit footballers for his American team, the Tampa Bay Rowdies. With Kempton Park only 11 miles from the centre of London he and his wife Nina had taken time off to come and cheer on their compatriot. It was a cold bleak day and any cheers in the vast stand echoed around the few spectators. The cheers resounded, though, when George came up into the final right-handed bend on the inside of one of the toughest professionals in the sport, Jeff King. The 'amateur' had cheekily gained the prize position on the rails. That looked good and when he asked Tiepolino to go on, he accelerated like a top racehorse to leave the favourites in his wake.

Not only was this a win, not only did this mean George joined Dick Saunders at the top of the Amateur table but Tiepolino had jumped superbly. The press were full of it the next day: 'Tiepolino jumped quite admirably throughout' – *The Daily Telegraph*; 'an immaculate display of fencing . . . Mr Sloan is an under-estimated jockey' – *The Times*.

Dick Saunders, however, did not take long to restore his superiority and take his tally to six. George thought his best chance of emulating him was through Mr Know All in an amateur chase at Wolverhampton. It meant a long trek from Findon to run at this Midlands track. Wolverhampton is a true surburban course lying in the midst of the millions of houses and factories of the Birmingham conurbation, with no scenic attractions. It is, however, a good track to ride and the fences are challenging – they are some of the biggest in England.

George's strongest opponent was once again Dick Saunders, who was getting plenty of rides

The Duchess of Norfolk presenting the trophy to George and his mother at Fontwell.

Worthing Herald, Friday, March 10, 1978 11

RACING DRAW FOR AMERICAN

Millionaire jets in for a year

AMERICAN millionaire George Sloan, who has made his home at High Salvington for a year to be near his 10 race horses at Josh Gifford's Findon stables, is riding high in this season's Amateur riders championship.

Story: Colin Clark
Photos:
Malcolm McCluskey

AMERICAN MILLIONAIRE owner-jockey George Sloan in the paddock at Fontwell last week.

With 12 winners to date, the 39-year-old owner jockey is three ahead of other riders.

Mr Sloan was born on a farm in Nashville, Tennessee. His parents owned several horses and were keen hunters.

Although he cannot recall the age at which he first rode, he remembers his first race at the age of 14, on his own mount, called Sunny Hour.

On leaving school he studied law at Vanderbilt University. He followed this profession for five years but spent spring and autumn weekends racing on the National Steeplechase and Hunt Association circuit.

At the age of 28 he became the president of a chain of 20 fried chicken restaurants. Two years later on selling the business he was established as a millionaire.

In 1968 his brother, Paul, came on a year's exchange visit to Lancing College where he taught English literature.

As a keen rider he contacted Ryan Price at his Findon stables and this led to both Paul and George riding in the 1969 Grand National. George's mount, Piccard, fell at Becher's on the first circuit.

Ryan Price bought seven
s from Ireland for Mr
and in 1970 former
pion jockey Josh Gif-
took over training
Price's steep
s.
tween 1973 an
Sloan made ab
a year to Fir
is horses being
to ride in
Association
1973 he had a
pt at the
nal on Fortu
d by Arthur
his American
er. This tir
ed the 18th fe
his mount fell.
bad fall at Sanc
put him in K
ital with a bro
his riding fut
.

Base

is happened onl
he had bought
at Mill Lane,
to use as a base
ermined attack
78 Amateur
hip.

GEORGE SLOAN on Mister Know All at F
week. It was one of his less successful races
second in a two-horse race to Persian Camp,
to Frankham.

year-old
Malcolm

three

The Nashville invader

Racing

by Brough Scott

DON'T think that those 1,352 lousy guitar-pickers are all they have in Nashville. They also have George Sloan, the 39-year-old health-spa-owner-cum-steeplechase-jockey who must surely be worth a song or two as he bids to become the first American to win Britain's amateur riders' title.

Last Monday, Sloan concluded that all racing over here was snowed off for at least a week, and so quit his riding base at Findon, Sussex, to wing back to Tennessee. Business thrived until Thursday, when a phone call from trainer Josh Gifford told Sloan that a thaw was under way and that his horse Tiepolino would run at Kempton on Friday, and so the boss of Cosmopolitan Spas Inc arrived red-eyed at Heathrow at nine o'clock on Friday morning, and won on

Tiepolino at two o'clock, having filled the intervening hours with a wedding reception at the Savoy.

Afterwards Sloan draped his beanpole figure ("I have been around 135 pounds since 1971") in a conservative grey suit. He still looked altogether better than during our last long conversation, nearly a year ago, when he was lying in Kingston Hospital with his leg so badly broken that many assumed his riding days were over.

Ironically enough, the day before that accident George had signed the contract for his present house at Findon as part of the assault plan on this season's amateur riders' championship. "I felt terrible then," he recalled on Friday. "But we had got so many nice horses together, and Josh was such a support and kept saying that there was no hurry, that I never really worried about setting this season up."

The Jubilee Sportsmen had put up some £50,000 of a total outlay of around £150,000, and few should have cause to regret it. For not only have Sloan's 11 winners so far put him ahead in his bid for the title, but the potential of the rest of his four-legged team could bring a fair return when they are all sold at the end of the season.

The present horse strength is 13. Ten are with Gifford at Findon, and three with George Fairbairn up in Northumberland, and just at the moment they look particularly worth watching. After riding Tiepolino on Friday and a promising novice, Jack Madness, at Stratford yesterday, Sloan moves on the Fontwell, Huntingd... Wetherby and Lingfield in th
next week.

Special note
the six horses t
hunter 'chases,
Boy, Mr. Fan
ground speciali
at Gifford's, an
Satanic Hymn a
are also eligibl
which Sloan ha
lems.

Such a catalo
that fun-loving
master of the N
shouldn't give
that the title
"OK, I've put
Sloan. "But it
get it for you.
for the disadva
the riding cont
the other boys

There is an
the Southern
you remember
has been riding
races for over 2
shuttling to E
Grand Nationa
worked himsel
after last year'
hard hours of
Findon

Maybe most
some would sa
of the market,
effort, accompli
then George Slo
horse he may
tomorrow. It's c
nessee.

Newton Abbot

FIRM GOING

*Allowance deducted

(bl) blinkers

1.45—TOTNES OPEN HUNTERS CHASE (Div I), of £836. 1st £530.60, 2nd £161.60, 3rd £77.80. Three miles two furlongs and 100 yards.

HELPEX ch g Parapex—Daily Help (M Davies) 10-11-12 ... Mr G Sloan 1
DEVON SPIRIT b g Spiritus—Seventh Symphony 13-12-0 (7*) ...Mr K Pook 2
ROMANY CHARM, b m Romany Air —unregistered 8-10-9 (7*) Miss P Ogden 3
Melivan, 8-10-9 (7*) Mr P Scudamore 4
Lava Star (bl), 11-11-5 (7*) Mr C Popham 5
Babuddin (bl), 10-10-9 (7*, car 11-1) Mr J de Lisle Wells 6
Eagle Moonday, 9-10-9 (7* car 10-11) Mr P Rawle 0
Patent, 8-11-2 (5*) ....Mr A Harris 0
Sunset Bay, 11-10-9 (7*) Mr E Hamner 0
Humperdinck, 8-11-2 ...Mr A J Wilson 0
Clear Horizon, 8-11-5 (7*, car 11-9)

5.17)
EWTON ABBOT CHALLENGE
P MAIDEN HURDLE (Div. II,
), of £970: 1st £657, 2nd
£87. Two miles and 150

VE b g Virginia Boy—Mere
ss J Waiwyn), 8-11-0 (5*)
K Mooney 1
b g Sira Dan—Brass Tacks
Mr G Sloan 2
b g Flandre II—Coronation
R B Evans 3
3-3 J Suthern 4
-10-13 (7*) Mr G Edwards 5

SLOAN HAS THE AMATEUR TITLE IN HIS GRASP

LEN THOMAS at FONTWELL

GEORGE SLOAN tightened his hold as leading amateur when notching his tenth winner of the season on Mister Know All in the Findon Handicap Chase at Fontwell yesterday.

The 32-year-old from Nashville, Tennessee, has set his heart on winning the amateur championship this season and with the horses

great stylist but his efforts seem highly effective.

He brought Mister Know All with a beautifully-timed challenge in the straight to cut down Flickity Prince on the run-in.

Flickity Prince, attempting to make all and fairly skipping over the obstacles, looked like staying in front until he began to tire approaching the second last.

He still held a fractional advantage at the last, but Mister
All displayed the better
speed on the flat to win
a length.

who came from a long
ck to win at Worcester
ight ago, left his effort
too late this time. He
d unsuited by this
figure of eight course.

DEBUT WIN

y, disappointing over
this season, made a pro-
winning first appear-
er fences in the Climp-
portunity Chase.

gelding took over when
ader Girton Girl blun-
the third and, making
emainder, stayed on
to hold off the persis-
ureen by half a length.

y, winner of four hurdle
tands no more than 16
nd seems a little small
sing, but he negotiated
nces in grand style and
uccesses should come

s bred by owner Martin
who still owns the six-
's dam, Noirmont Girl,
at the Tedfold Stud
the service of Derby
Morston.

SLOAN SWOOPS AS PENNY DROPS TOO LATE!

REPORT FROM NEWTON ABBOT

PENNY OGDEN yesterday joined the illustrious list of jockeys who have miscounted the circuits in a race at Newton Abbot.

She rode a finish a lap too soon and pulled up on Romany Charm, favourite in the first division of the Totnes Open Hunters Chase.

When the others sailed by her she rallied her mount, but the damage was done and she finished only third to Helpex. 21st winner of the season for leading amateur George Sloan.

The embarrassed Miss Ogden was cautioned by the stewards for not acquainting herself with the course.

Owner Mark Davies, a commodity broker from Sussex, has won point-to-points on Helpex, but he gave the mount here to his friend George Sloan to help him clinch the amateurs' title.

Sussex permit-holder Chris Wates sent out his first double with Moonstone Lass and September Rain, both partnered by Peter Haynes.

Moonstone Lass got the first instalment of the maiden hurdle on the disqualification of Charlton Fox, who finished first on merit but veered across Moonstone Lass on the flat.

So Susan Morris stays on the 13 mark. She said: "It's usually a lucky number for me, but this could be a blessing in disguise. Charlton Fox is only a baby and it means he is still a novice for the start of next season."

September Rain, running for the second time in 19 hours, steadily cut down Transformation's long lead to jump ahead at the last in the Washington Singer Memorial Challenge Cup.

He had finished fourth to Party Line the previous evening at Ludlow after stumbling on the last bend.

Wates left the decision about running again to Miss Mardy Nance, who looks after his horses, so she was relieved and delighted.

Odds-on favourite Clifton Fair, fourth, could not stride out on the firm ground.

Jackie Thorne, 24-year-old daughter of Bridgwater trainer John, notched her second riding success of the meeting with another forceful display on Penny Orange.

This time she was sporting the Otter Way colours of Oliver

Continued on back page

from his many supporters in his Championship bid. This time his horse was Ireland's Owen, who went into the last fence neck and neck with Mr Know All. There was nobody else with a chance, only the two main contenders for the Championship. It was an extra challenge. George could not let Dick get further ahead, he had to take the risk and he asked Mr Know All for the big stand back. The horse tried, leapt high but just clipped the top of the fence as he was coming down. That was enough to unbalance him, head his nose into the ground and jettison him into a spectacular somersault. Horse and jockey lay still for a few seconds, but then hobbled to their feet – George with blood all over his face was in reasonable shape, but Mr Know All hardly dared put his badly cut hind legs to the ground.

More gloom for George, as ahead Dick had galloped past the winning post – to notch up seven wins and a lead of two; and at his side, Mr Know All, one of his most courageous and successful partners looked too hurt to race again that season.

Whether it was to offer George some consolatory fun, or whether it was a calculated effort to get rid of his rival, Dick Saunders invited George for a day with the Pytchley Foxhounds of which he was Master. George knowing Dick to be one of those few people who, although intensely competitive, was still warm, friendly and thoughtful, decided to take the risk. New Arctic was boxed up from Huntingdon and together they survived the day without being trapped in any ditches.

George began to relax, not to be on the look out for any snares from his rival, with the result he was caught fair and square by the cellar. At the hospitable Saunderses' dinner-party, with the aid of the stimulants from the cellar, George's spirits rose higher and higher, the stories got better and better, and one guest was heard to murmur: 'great stories but I do not know where I could possibly tell them!'

It was the next morning when the alarm went off at 6 am that George found out the seriousness of the alcoholic trap into which he had fallen. His trip South and his day with the Crawley and Horsham foxhounds qualifying his hunter chasers, was a painful experience.

December

In bitterness the heart recalls
The chances thrown away.
OGILVIE

George heralded in December with that awful hangover acquired with the Saunderses. It is a month which gives trainers plenty of headaches for the British weather starts to try out its range of tricks. Meetings are usually called off through frost, or fog, rain or snow during this unpredictable month; adversities that usually occur at the last possible moment, and trainers often have their horses plated (light shoes to replace the harder wearing heavy ones), and even on the road to the meeting, before that ominous announcement on the radio news: 'Racing has been abandoned at . . .' During the deep winter months the weather becomes a vital factor in training. A race is picked out for a horse, he is prepared especially for it, the entries appear beatable, and then it is cancelled.

Tiepolino at Sandown was George's first ride in December. There was some anxiety as the weather became crisper but there was not enough frost in the ground to stop Sandown's Saturday meeting. The Esher track had been one of George's favourite courses, at least until he broke his leg there just nine months before. It is an exhilarating course to ride on a good jumper, but a hair-raising one on a poor performer. There is an awkward downhill plain fence which the horses usually approach on their forehand and can only launch themselves into the air if well-balanced. Then there are the six fences along the backside – the famous railway straight – elating when they came right, hairy if a horse meets one wrong. The last bit of path to glory or failure is a long uphill climb which saps the energy of all but the most courageous stayers. But George's ride, Tiepolino, sailed over all those tricky fences to win his second chase and take George to just one win behind Dick Saunders.

George's ambitions to take over that lead were fired the following week as he was asked to the Bollinger dinner. This was the evening of the champions when they were presented with their trophies, made their speeches and received a little of the honour and glory their efforts deserved. The Amateur Champion, Peter Greenall, had had to rest on his laurels. After three years of chasing titles and finally winning one outright he had been devoting his time to his family's brewing interests – Greenall Whitney. He had not been seen in a race since his victory and by the size of his girth it seemed as if he had been indulging himself at business lunches. The popular professional Champion,

Tommy Stack, had more than a rounder tummy to restrict his riding for he was in a wheelchair. This was his first night out from Hexham Hospital where he had been strung up in traction since September. Such are the ups and downs of a jump jockey's life.

George had one of the 'ups' the next day; not only did he have the morale booster of being offered his first decent outside ride, on a horse called Yellow Fire, but he won by 12 lengths. Pat Rohan was the man who telephoned with the offer, one week before: 'They say you are trying to win the championship. I would like to help and have a ride for you at Newcastle'. It was startling news, for the first and last time George had met Pat Rohan was 10 years before in the hunting field with the West Waterford Foxhounds, but few Irishmen forget sporting acquaintances and fortunately Pat Rohan was not one of them.

George would not be hunting in Ireland this year; his approach to the Championship was a straight line course – no diversions or unnecessary risks of injury. This practice was not always followed as two former Champions, Chris Collins (1965/66 and 1966/67) and Peter Greenall (joint 1975/76 and outright 1976/77) told him they took time off to go ski-ing. George learnt about their tactics at a dinner which Chris Collins gave in December. Advice was thrown at him including some that made him smart – 'Never risk the horses at the beginning of the season' – and George thought about the three horses that would be unlikely to run again in his campaign because of his haste.

George accepted some of this advice but he realized they had all used tactics to suit their different temperaments. Basically George considers himself an instinctive campaigner launching into ventures with all guns firing. He would not carry out the thorough Collins studies of each situation. George summed it all up by saying: 'I would not be as good at flying by instruments as Chris, I am better at flying by the seat of my pants'. The cocky young Greenall, who just happened to be good at most things he did, would be closer to this latter category, but the three shared one asset – a ruthless will to win.

That will to win did not help George in his next two rides. Both Tiepolino and Dark Spectre, a horse bought unseen from Ireland, failed to get past the post first. George, however, thought he had one certainty as Pat Rohan had asked him to ride his Newcastle winner Yellow Fire at the Yorkshire track of Catterick. Business, however, was clamouring for his return; so he headed across the Atlantic for the weekend but was back, eager to head North on Tuesday morning. He set off towards that rough country course knowing that he and Yellow Fire had beaten most of their opponents at Newcastle. The only difference was an extra half-mile and that was what told, for soon after George headed into the straight looking like a winner the others started flying by. The 'dead cert' had been beaten and George had a six-hour drive back to Findon to cogitate about the uncertainties of racing.

Then, for the first time in George's season there were four days without a single race meeting. Christmas had called a halt to proceedings but to make up for this interlude eight meetings were staged on Boxing Day. That was a day to get the winners that George direly needed, especially as another opponent had reared his sporting head to join George and Dick Saunders in the lead. His name was Mark Brisbourne and although lacking his own supply of horses he was young, tough, talented, and good enough to turn professional when he wanted to. Because of these attributes he was getting a very large number of rides, and George knew he could be a real danger.

Over the weekend George and Josh churned through the entries, looked up the form of all likely opponents, rang up trainers to see if they were going to run. It was another of those time-consuming, systematic analyses of which horse or horses to run and where. They finally came up with the race that was furthest away, 300 miles north on the beautifully built galloping course of Wetherby. Tiepolino was the horse, and on Christmas Day he was shipped off to face what, on paper, appeared to be mediocre opposition.

Tiepolino started hot favourite, and jockey and backers were happy as he approached the last fence in the lead, but then George relaxed. The horse thought he could too, and before George could rustle him him up again the second came flying by. The crowd booed, George knew he had made a terrible mistake. Another of his 'dead certs' had lost and this time through his own error – it made that long journey home very painful. The only compensation came from the racing results for although all his amateur rivals were riding favourites none had won.

It was short-term compensation as with the unusually low tally of seven winners for the amateur leaders, the young title holder Peter Greenall, who had the two best qualifications – talent and funds – thought he must have a chance. He had spent six months being serious in business and now he was tempted to try and to join the title race at this very late stage.

George knew of this danger, that Brisbourne could muster up many more rides, and that Saunders's best rides came in the spring with the hunter chases which are confined to amateur riders. George was desperate once more; none of his horses in training had a race in them for a fortnight or so – they had all spent their energy, had coughs or were injured. He headed off to Ireland on another buying escapade, but could only find one horse – a £13,000 five year-old called Jack Madness who he bought from Tommy Kinane.

George than flew across the Atlantic to bury his head in business and try to forget that he should be racing horses that were not there to ride.

Riding out in the winter.

January

If you can meet with Triumph and Disaster
And treat those two impostors just the same.

KIPLING

January can be the gloomiest month in the British racing calendar. The odd days of racing abandoned in December often turn into weeks in this inhospitable month. Those meetings that are held test the endurance of racegoers, trainers, jockeys and horses against hard frosts, hock deep going, icy winds, frequent soakings and occasional banks of fog. But for George there were some silver linings.

On Friday the 13th, Josh called him in America, there was a good race for Tiepolino three days ahead. George packed his bags and within 24 hours was flying for the thirteenth

Tiepolino establishes himself as one of the season's best novices with this win at Chepstow.

time that season across the Atlantic. It was no easy race, he had to take on Levantine who had won six consecutive races. The course was Chepstow, which lay across the Severn river in Wales. This is one of the most picturesque but testing tracks, for there were hardly any straight flat sections, the track rose, fell and twisted its way through the luscious Welsh country; but Tiepolino excelled, and galloped away with this £2,000 race. George had gained the lead in the Championship race for the first time.

They had only just got that race in in time. Heavy rains forced the abandonment of racing until the weekend when the gravel base of Kempton came into its own – that ground is rarely waterlogged.

A novice hurdle at Kempton was chosen as the début for Pride of Tennessee, the horse George had bought as an unbroken four-year-old more than a year before. The first race track trial of a young horse is nerve-wracking – is the money wasted?; will he jump?; can he accelerate?; has he the temperament? – are questions answered in a few exciting minutes. Pride of Tennessee came out all trumps as far as George was concerned. He was green, but he jumped nimbly, gathered speed when asked, and only faded when tired at the end.

The elation of discovering that this was a good horse showed in George's big grin as he rode up to Josh in the unsaddling area. The happy spirits were not mutual. 'I am not a bit pleased with that', said the trainer. 'You made far too much use of him. He might not run for two months.' Probably George would have got his horse more relaxed about racing if he had not asked him to make any effort, but he did run a very impressive fourth just two weeks later.

Two days later George galloped Tiepolino through the mud at Worcester, the track on the edge of the River Severn to chalk up his ninth win of the season. That felt good but it was no guarantee of the Championship as Mark Brisbourne scored again.

Non-racing activities include chopping wood for Josh's and George's fires.

February

Be thine enemy an ant, see him as an elephant
TURKISH PROVERB

In February there is hope, spring lies in the foreseeable future, the tracks dare to stage more major races as there is less fear of abandonment. The meetings also acquire a fresh set of races and racegoers with the start of the hunter chases. These races, confined to amateur riders on horses that have been fairly hunted, bring on to the racecourse the real sports many of whom hunt, train and race their own hunter chaser.

Seven of George's horses had been gently hunted that winter, to qualify for the hunter chases. Previous Amateur Champions had used these races as a good means of picking up wins. Ironically, not one of George's horses succeeded in a hunter chase, although they won handicap chases and hurdle races.

George's next winner was his old friend Mr Know All who had miraculously recovered from his damaging Worcester fall in November. He galloped away with his third race of the season, his second at the local Fontwell track.

The weather messed up further plans – this time the frost not the rain. George waited one week for the freeze up to end then hopped on a plane to attend to some more business in Tennessee. Few useful operations could be completed for within 24 hours there was a call from Josh. 'The weather is breaking. Tiepolino has a good chance at Kempton on Friday.' One day later George was back again, just in time for the morning wedding of his great friend and supporter, Henry Pelham, to another ardent racegoer Sarah Charlton. George arrived bleary-eyed in the early hours of Friday morning, changed and headed to the Savoy Chapel, changed and headed to Kempton racecourse, changed and rode Tiepolino to win. There were celebrations for George and celebrations for Josh who won a crate of champagne as Kempton's leading trainer. Nor did all this pass over the heads of the newly-weds as there was a telegram in the weighing room: 'Well done the church must do you good'.

There might have been celebrations in the Sloan camp but another organization was building up ambitions on the title. It was a camp that could not be taken lightly for it was responsible for the previous season's amateur and professional champions and in a number of the years before that. It was Arthur Stephenson whose Bishop Auckland stable holds the record for the largest number of winners produced in any one season. A maestro at producing winners, Stephenson had adopted as his protégé a young teenager – Geordie Dun, the son of a Scottish farmer. The plan was to attack the Championship in 1978–79 but when the stable jockey Tommy Stack shattered his pelvis, and when the Scottish farmer's son proved he was learning fast, Stephenson persuaded more of his owners to give the 'amateur' a ride. The winners started accumulating and everyone knew that if Stephenson wanted to make him the Champion, then there seemed little that George's horsepower could do against the might of that yard.

There were more and more signs that Stephenson did want to make Dun the champ, there were even sinister rumours that he had put a large bet on his protégé to win the title. Dick Saunders and Mark Brisbourne the early leaders might appear beaten; Peter Greenall had never really got into the swing; but now at this late stage George realized a much more serious rival had started his challenge.

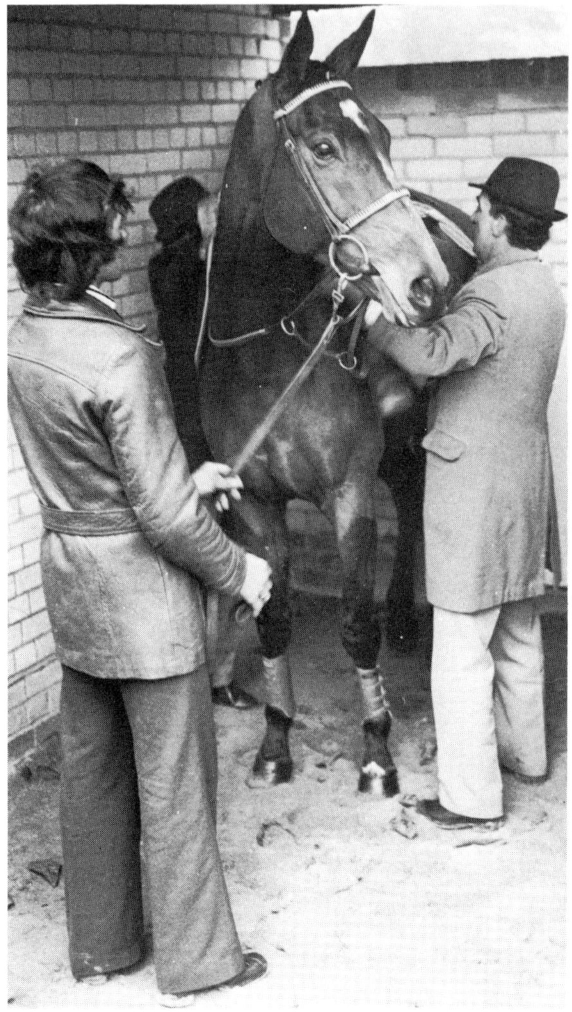

Josh saddles up with the assistance of head travelling lad, Snowy, and Mr Know All's lad, Gary.

March

Golden hopes that come to guide us
Splendid dreams that float beside us;
Aintree calls!
OGILVIE

March is the month of climaxes in the British National Hunt season. It is the month when the most talented horses and jockeys test their skills against the best in Britain and Ireland at the Cheltenham Festival meeting. It is the month when the brave and greatest jumpers risk their 'hearts' and health over those massive Aintree fences. These are the events for which the trainers prepare, jockeys angle for rides, and racegoers organize their holidays – but not George. At these the two greatest meetings of the year he was a frustrated spectator. He had the horses and he longed to be out there on the track at Cheltenham having a cut at the most prestigious races of the year. At Aintree he only had to walk on the course to look at those enormous manicured fences and to feel shivers down his spine. He wanted to ride, but this year he needed quantity not quality and that meant keeping to the less competitive races at the less important courses.

One such race was a maiden hunter chase at the Lincolnshire track of Market Rasen. Restricted to amateur riders on horses that had been fairly hunted and unsuccessful on the race track it seemed ideal for Choral Prince – the little horse George Fairbairn trained which had fallen last time out when well placed to win.

This race on this straightforward but rather bleak course in the midst of a 1,000 acre wild life sanctuary, seemed perfect for him. It was the only race of the year George was temped to bet on himself, for Choral Prince's price was long with 'OOF' form behind him. Choral Prince jumped so brilliantly that he pulled himself to the front in time for the open ditch. He met it all wrong, rapped the guard rail on the way up, and had to put in a cat-like leap to stay on his feet; a very clever horse but he catapulted his jockey out of the saddle.

From then on there were clear bits, hazy moments and blank times in George's memory of events. He had hit his head and although he made the weighing-room on his feet, a short conversation with George Fairbairn's new wife Liz had her racing to find his co-driver Macer Gifford: 'George is goofy. Get him home quickly'. Macer knew if the doctors saw George was suffering from concussion he would be automatically banned from riding for a week. Macer knew too that George would take any risk when good rides were at stake and there were three in just two days' time. He raced to save him from the hands of those who cared more for his health than winning the Championship, collected him in his car and took him home to Huntingdon.

George was a sensible patient the next day, but then he felt pretty sick. He rested, spent two hours with a masseuse to help his stiff aching neck – but on the Monday he was off again.

Two of the rides were not worth the risk for Crofter and Mr Fantasy were returning to the racetrack after more than two years on the sidelines. They needed a few races to get into top condition and found it difficult to heave through the deep going at the Midlands track of Leicester. But his old colleague Mr Know All for the fourth time that year got past the post first.

That needed some celebrating and George was, after all, passing his favourite spot for rest and recreation on the way home. This was the Bridge Hotel at Huntingdon where good food, lively music and most important of all – an unusually high standard of lady assistants made it a gathering point for all the bachelors in the vicinity.

George did not go alone, for Josh's new assistant trainer the meticulous, ultraconscientious Anton Pearson was acting as co-driver. George however, after the excitement of enjoying his success amongst the ladies of the Bridge Hotel thought it would be a good idea to have more company on the long journey back to Findon. One sporting pretty lady was persuaded that it would be fun to drive for hours through the night to Sussex.

George decided to minimize this driving time, put his foot on the floorboards of his BMW coupé and made London in less than one hour. The lady might have appreciated this reduction in driving time, but this reckless approach to life had shaken the rather more sober and certainly less foolhardy assistant trainer.

George however, enjoys trying to convert the well behaved to the excitements of a faster life. His education of Anton that night included giving chase through the streets of London to a Porsche that had bumped into the back of his BMW, and a midnight call on friends to wake the lady of the house from her slumbers.

George escaped unhurt from the dangers of that evening but more trouble lay ahead. When about to start his breakfast with the Giffords in the morning he was told that another of his lady friends was riding out second lot. Feeling more discreet in the morning air he hastily retreated to his house, took lady number one to the train, and returned to give lady number two an all-innocent welcome. The lads, Anton, Josh and Althea had as much fun out of his morning dash around as George did with his evening's education of Anton.

George had a couple of days to recover from this escapade before his favourite meeting of the year – the Grand Military at Sandown. He was fond of it because the unusual races confined to amateurs, and past and present members of the forces brought a sporting international group of riders and spectators to this London track. He had too prepared his purchase out of the Cork Hospital, Super Travel, especially for Saturday's Past and Present Hurdle; but at a cocktail party given by National Hunt's most beloved patron, The Queen Mother, he found

Josh talks to his assistant Anton Pearson.

out that the Swede, Major Lars Swaerd, had also trained his horse, Tammers For, especially for that same race. The rest of the horses could be discounted but Tammers For had enough class to be the runner-up in the previous year's Imperial Cup.

The American and Swedish jockeys spent Friday evening discussing their chances at the Royal cocktail party and later over dinner. The next day they found themselves coming into the last hurdle neck and neck, but it was George's game young Super Travel who struggled to get the lead from the hot favourite Tammers For. That was a thrilling win for George who proved he had a very good horse indeed to a large and distinguished group of racegoers.

The memory of those moments of glory were some help the following week as Tiepolino fell at the second last when hot favourite in a race at Newcastle. George had to spend six hours in the car nursing a bruised backside, thinking about the wasted effort of that long journey, and remembering that it was his main rival, Geordie Dun, who won the race after Tiepolino's failure.

Still there was Easter, and with 12 meetings on the Monday, there had to be some easy races. They found one for little Pride of Tennessee at Wincanton who made his first contribution to George's Championship bid; but Super Travel disappointed in his début over the big fences, jumping greenly and finishing third. That meant George was all square with Dun, who also managed just one winner.

Next Saturday was a difficult ordeal, for that was when George wanted to be taking on those intoxicating Aintree fences and instead he had to go to Towcester to ride in ordinary races. It was however a lovely course in the midst of Lord Hesketh's Northamptonshire estate. The circuit was a long one with steep hills that test a horse's stamina and galloping powers. It became even more lovely in George's eyes when Mr Know All, taking on the flying American horse, Tingle Creek, and the very consistent Perambulate, upset the odds and won. Towcester looked almost as good as Aintree after Crofter, who had been almost tailed off, kept gamely running on and aided by his jockey's unorthodox but spirited finishing style just got up to win, completing a double for George.

Pride of Tennessee in a novice hurdle at Newbury.

April

And away and away and away they went,
A visible song of what life meant,
Living in houses, sleeping in bed,
Going to business, all seemed dead,
Dead as death to that rush in strife,
Pulse for pulse with the heart of life.

MASEFIELD

April is a month of anti-climax for the Grand National marks the end of National Hunt domination of the racing scene. The jumpers are squeezed out on to the country tracks, with the odd big race slotted in between flat races at the major tracks. The only things that really count now are the Championships, and for those that are contesting them there are still two months of travelling to courses all over the country, riding out every day, analysing the form to place the horses in the best races, and searching for rides. This month the glamour can cloud a little with racing at the colourful big meetings finished and the excitements of the end of the season yet so far ahead.

George was not letting up – he even bought another horse from his friend Mark Davies, a commodity broker and point-to-point rider. The horse – Sir Tacks – did not stay the three miles of point-to-points but was bred to manage the two miles of the novice chases. He was, however, pigeon-toed, hobdayed and had never won; but George rode him in a muddy field and liked him enough to pay what he thought was way above his market value £4,500.

He then headed north followed in trains and hired cars by a large contingent of American supporters. He knew they were in for a treat because he was racing at Hexham, a course overlooking the wild Northumberland countryside. The natural setting is so magnificent that it magnifies the exhiliration of any successes, and minimizes the disasters. On this occasion there were social festivities planned by the hospitable Fairbairns and Allendale family. A dinner party on Saturday, and a lunch lasting five hours were to give the Americans a warm taste of aristocratic British hospitality.

Hexham was a new course to George and he was walking it during the first race praying that his close rival Dun, who was on the favourite might get beaten. Unhappily the young Scotsman's horse complied with George's wishes rather too vigorously, falling and giving his jockey a broken collarbone. That was the luck of the game, this time it was Geordie another time it would be George. But the American had to admit that at least the gods of injury had made up for last year's broken leg by remaining on his side this season. It was not only Geordie Dun who had suffered; George's other main rival Nick Henderson's attack on the title had been hampered by a dislocated shoulder then a broken collar bone, and the year before by broken vertebrae. Championship bidders need to pray to the god of health.

At Hexham George was riding the horse that had given him his worst fall of the year – that knock on the head at Market Rasen. Choral Prince, however, settled happily in the sunshine and to racing over the lower hurdles. He coasted up the steep hill whilst the others were being driven along draining them of that precious energy. George waited confidently at the rear asked for a late run from his little horse and sailed by a big field of maiden runners.

Over the Saturday night and Sunday came the great festivities at the Fairbairns and Allendales for all the Americans. Then the ride on Yellow Fire on Monday.

George was sailing near the wind and he employed equally daring tactics on the second day of the meeting when riding Yellow Fire for Pat Rohan. He brought it off again and the Irish trainer told the press: 'He's a confident rider for an amateur. I thought Lester Piggot was bad but this fellow is worse'.

Yellow Fire's win brought the tally to 18, but George knew he could not get complacent, he might be well ahead of the injured Dun but there was another worry on the horizon – the most 'professional' of all the amateurs – Jim Wilson. This amusing, tough equine swimming-pool manager was getting most of the injured Nick Henderson's high-class rides. Jim's threat kept George on his toes. He dashed South after Hexham, driving through the night and a freak April snowstorm to make two rides at Plumpton the next day. They were placed but missed the highest honours as he did during the following days on Captain George, Tiepolino, Mr Fantasy and Super Travel.

For three weeks he did everything but win and the dread began to creep in that this could be a repeat performance of his American Amateur Title chase. Then he had driven all over America, taken every ride he could engineer, but to no avail; in the last two-and-a-half months of the season he failed to get a single winner.

An old friend was able to reassure him that such an extraordinary run cannot happen twice, for at the end of April Mr Fantasy won his first race after his two-and-a-half year lay-off. It was excellent timing for Mr Fantasy's owner, the newly married Susie Chatfield Taylor, flew over for the weekend. She had managed to persuade her husband Wayne, who, as an architect, was more interested in buildings than horses, that it would be worth a trip across the Atlantic to see her horse run.

Wayne did not have a chance to look at many buildings too closely as they spent most of their time in a car travelling across half of England to get to the Lincolnshire course of Market Rasen; but Mr Fantasy, did his best to make it worthwhile by beating the hot favourite, Arctic Challenge. This success gave George a double boost for it made one of his favourite owners happy, and there was a saga behind the beaten horse.

The main opposition, Arctic Challenge, had come out of the stable of George's own trainer, George Fairbairn. In normal times he would have enjoyed the challenge of trying to achieve a difficult victory, but as a title chaser every win is far too vital. He knew too that a sporting custom had been defied for supporters of jockeys going for a Championship try to avoid running horses against them. Not knowing that George Fairbairn had tried but was unable to persuade the owner/rider of Arctic Challenge to run elsewhere, George had been distressed, but his unexpected win provided a happy end to the incident, and to the month of April.

The Faces of a Champion.

May

Brushing the birches come three of 'em over it –
Stirrup to stirrup, locked level they land;
Sit down and ride em!

OGILVIE

In May, racing acquires more of a holiday spirit. The serious business is over. The good horses are gorging themselves on the spring grass, holidaying in the fields after their winter work. It is the turn of the less valuable hard ground gallopers who run for small prizes at the country tracks. For most, a win is merely an end of season bonus, but at Findon there was a much more serious spirit. The stables were still full of horses for Josh was after the Trainers Championship and George the Amateur crown.

George, however, was well enough ahead to become a trifle confident and take time off to go racing in the States. It was his home race, the Iroquois, that he wanted to win for the fifth time, and he had a great chance on the English import, Charlie Murphy.

George boarded the aeroplane a little less confidently having just heard that Geordie Dun had recovered from his broken collarbone well enough to ride a winner. In Nashville, George's worries were forgotten for he arrived to a blaze of publicity and great public expectancy about the chances of the current leader in the British Amateur Championship. His good spirits were not enhanced in the race for the horse he hoped would be a Grand National prospect broke down at the second last.

So, with no luck in the USA, he beat a hasty retreat to the UK but there was no comfort there. He arrived in time to go out to dinner and was greeted by an unhappy looking Henry Pelham: 'I have very bad news for you. Dun had a double today'. Within a week the Scottish teenager had come from six behind to within three wins of George's total, and he was riding a favourite on the next day.

How quickly the situation had changed and it made George think about the Championship story of two years before. Then in the last two weeks Peter Greenall had five winners to come from behind and share the title. He, like Geordie Dun, depended on Arthur Stephenson to produce this stream of winners.

The chase was really on now, and the next morning when George got off the London/Perth sleeper train he found the press had been quick to pick up this new swing in the Championship race. He had travelled through the night for a ride at this Scottish city's beautiful track, in a race in which Dun was riding the favourite. He walked the course examining the contours, the bends, the going, and barely noticing the magnificence of the venerable trees and river which wound along this park course. He could not shut out the thought of what losing would be like, of having the achievement of his ambition snatched away at this late stage. He had to win, and then of all people he bumped into the burly figure of the man with the key to the Championship Arthur Stephenson. 'Take it easy on my little boy', the horsedealer-cum-farmer-cum-trainer said, with just a hint of a twinkle in his wily eyes. George laughed but could not suppress a more serious tone when he replied: 'Your little boy has plenty of time to win the Championship'. A sense of humour becomes harder to muster when dreams look as if they could be snatched away.

This battle with Dun was becoming deadly serious. There were none of the laughs between them, and little of that competitive camaraderie that were features of George's relationships with his other older rivals. The Scottish teenager was aware of Stephenson's faith in him and it was a burden that made it difficult to get on with his competitor as well as he did before and after the title race.

Geordie must have found it very difficult to laugh that day at Perth. He rode the favourite confidently on to the corner of the bend into the back stretch, but got squeezed backwards and then lost his irons when the horse made a bad mistake – his bold tactics lost him the race. George's mount Choral Prince, though, flew past the post and that Scottish crowd cheered the jockey who was beating their local lad in the Championship race. The sporting ovation of the Scottish people; the elation, after the fear of being caught, meant that George left Perth feeling about two feet taller than when he had arrived.

George's horses were entered everywhere in the remaining two-and-a-half weeks of the season. At all costs he had to be able to counter a last minute spurt from the Dun/Stephenson partnership. He had three rides at a Warwick

Working up the sand.

evening meeting – with no results. Back to Findon and then a 400-mile round trip for another evening meeting at Nottingham, only to just get beaten.

Then it was down to the seaside at Newton Abbot where the shabbiness of the track was made up for by the sunshine, the high spirits of holidaymakers, and the stalls selling those revolting-looking, but delicious, jellied eels. The horses were made to work hard in this frantic end of the season 'keep on top' effort. Captain George ran on both days of this two-day meeting as did George's most recent purchase, Sir Tacks. Frustratingly, neither quite made it. George's horses earned him three seconds and a third that would sound pretty good to most people, but not to him when only winners counted.

He did, however, find a winner. Sir Tacks's former owner Mark Davies kept his point-to-pointers in training with the 1955 Gold Cup hero, Tony Grantham. This retired jockey who used to ride The Queen Mother's steeple-chasers had also looked after George's horses that were lame tired or were in the early stages of getting fit. Grantham and Mark decided it would be sporting to help George's title bid and to give him the ride on Mark's point-to-pointer Helpex. The gesture was appreciated and fruitful for he was George's 21st winner of the season.

One day's rest; then it was off to Towcester where Crofter, running in his 10th race of the season won very impressively. Mr Fantasy only just missed a victory after making a mistake at the water so he was boxed up and driven the 250 miles up to Hexham. Travelling for miles, asking the horses to run, run and run again – all had to be tried for Dun had six good rides at the Bank Holiday meeting of Cartmel. The opposition there would be very poor and with luck on his side, it was not impossible to win them all; at least that was what the over-anxious championship leader thought.

Mr Fantasy could not help: he ran second, as did Choral Prince on that vital Bank Holiday Monday when he was supposed to be a 'dead cert' at Huntingdon. But the despondency caused by Choral Prince's narrow defeat did not last for long; a telephone call to Cartmel brought the best news George had all season – Dun had only one winner. Barring a miracle, the Championship had to be his.

There were no celebrations, but in the final five days of the 1977/78 season the high spirits in the Sloan camp were hard to suppress. Josh, too, was feeling good for even though he had lost his champion trainer's race – both Fred Winter and Arthur Stephenson overtaking him in the final weeks – it was still his best ever season.

Jockies celebrating at George and Jane's wedding.
From left to right, standing: *Bob Champion, Dick Saunders, George Sloan and Jim Wilson.*
Sitting: *Anthony Webber, Macer Gifford and Mason Lampton* (USA)

June

Fifty guineas! – So that's the end
of a rattling ride and a right good friend.

OGILVIE

June is traditionally England's most glorious month and it really lived up to its reputation in 1978. Until late May persistent rains had swamped all efforts by the plants to grow. When the sun finally broke through nature burst forth, the trees quickly coating themselves in luminiscent green, the flowers and blossom splurging the countryside in magnificent colour. It all seemed extra special after the months and months of dreary greyness.

While it was a privilege to be allowed to see nature at her most ravishing, even if it had been raining George Sloan would have felt good, for on the third day of that glorious month he achieved his goal.

On the last day of the season he rode Crofter at Stratford-upon-Avon to win his 23rd race of the year and secure the Championship.

There was, as there had been for most of the season, a large contingent of his countrymen to cheer him on. There were his parents, his partner Seth Smith, who had shouldered the work to make this venture possible; and there was the most enthusiastic syndicate member the delicate Ginny Swaeb.

Americans plus British supporters, plus trainer made up a large contingent of participants in the Sloan victory celebrations. A convoy of four cars set off on the three-hour trip from Stratford but on this occasion it took nearly double the accustomed time. The extra hours were spent savouring one of those rare and happy moments of achievement; and the best way of doing that is over a drink with those most involved, recalling the funny, bad and glorious times on the way to success. An abundance of attractive pubs along the road south meant there were no problems in holding these frequent discussions about George's year.

The destination was a tiny old Tudor restaurant with some of the best food in the South of England. Friends had already heard, for there were telegrams and champagne awaiting the new champion. It was the start of a week of celebrating that tested the endurance powers of the Champion Amateur to the limit.

On the Sunday, Nick and Valda Embiricos offered compensation for one of Valda's horses twice running against George and twice beating him in close finishes, by laying on a sumptuous lunch. The exuberant 'champ' was cheeky enough to throw his smartly-dressed mother fully clad into the swimming pool; and crazy enough to lay bets with the former point-to-point rider, Brian Trafford, that he could jump a 4 ft 6 in high and 4 ft wide hedge. Without the help of his horse he found it only possible to jump through not over such a hedge but he emerged unscathed, ready for more fun.

Monday night was his beaten rival Nick Henderson's bachelor party. It had an unusual ending; after the traditional boozy dinner and joke telling sessions, Nick took them on to Annabel's night club, not to have his last fling with floozy ladies but to meet his fiancée Diana Thorne and some of her friends. This appeared to be a clever bit of feminine guile to prevent the evening from becoming too out of hand; but for George it had unforeseen consequences. He took Nick's future sister-in-law Jane Thorne – Diana's twin and, like her, a talented jockey – on to the dance floor, looked into her eyes and felt enough of those romantic stirrings to start wondering. Six months later, George had stopped wondering, was quite sure, and asked Jane to be his wife.

George and Jane on their wedding day.

This alcoholic and romantic evening did not make the next day any easier to get through. It was Ascot Sales, the day when everyone of his equine partners in the title race were going under the auctioneer's hammer. It was intended to be a financial bonanza, a means of repaying all the Americans who had helped back his venture. It was a logical and sensible move but gruelling on the emotions to have to get rid of so many sources of excitement and fun. With each fall of the hammer and 'sold to . . .' the feeling of loss became worse. The dreams, the planning, the preparation, the struggle, the fun had been fruitful, but they were all over. This ruthless farewell to his partners resulted in anti-climax getting the upper hand on the euphoria of victory.

The money, however, poured in. It was the most successful sale in Ascot's history. £21,000 was paid for Tiepolino the cornerstone of the Championship and the five-time winner; £17,000 for Super Travel, the horse with so much talent who had been bought out of Cork hospital; £16,500 for Sir Tacks, the horse who quadrupled his value in two months despite not winning a single race; £16,000 for Choral Prince, who had compensated George for the headache he gave him with two impressive wins; £12,000 for Jack Madness, who looked so promising but had not had time to acclimatize; £10,400 for Con Hurley, who gave him his very first win; £9,400 for the brave Mr Know All who despite bad injuries won five races; £6,400 for Crofter, who kept running better and better; £5,200 for the magnificent Jubilee Sportsman, who hit his fetlock in the hunting field and never ran; £2,600 for Captain George, whose running changed so much that George had to explain it to the stewards; £2,300 for Mr Fantasy, who had given George some of his earliest wins in England; £2,200 for Darke Spectre, the horse he bought unseen and never won; £2,400 for Castlegay, the horse he was keen to run too early

The Sloan campaign horses parading before being auctioned at Ascot Sales.

and jarred his tendons on the hard going; £1,900 for Dream and Scheme, the horse whose talents were ruined by a virus that affected his wind; £900 for his favourite Monfire, whose legs now looked only strong enough for hunting; and £720 for London Light, the Irish mare with good form but who had broken down and bled. These 16 horses made George, the syndicate and his friends £126,920 the richer but drained some of the fun out of the victory.

George badly needed a morale booster and so a quiet dinner in London with his parents, George Fairbairn and a few friends was decided upon. These were some of George's best behaved friends and relations, but they were not quiet enough for the Chelsea restaurant, La Famiglia, which complained about the noise and eventually asked them to leave. The Sloan seniors did not know whether to be indignant about this criticism or pleased that they had been naughty enough to be reprimanded like youngsters. Anyway they certainly enjoyed the next stage of the evening – the night club – before the trip home.

George went on to pick up Josh from the eve of the Derby Dinner and was greeted by his trainer's demand for £300. It was to be George's share in a Derby runner of which he had never heard. That, thought George, was a generous donation to charity. The next day he turned on the television to watch the Derby and routed hard for his compatriot, Willie Shoemaker. He did, however, think he recognized the name of the horse that got up and beat the American jockey. He checked and sure enough Shirley Heights was on the ticket. That gave him an extra £1,760 for celebrations, and even more reason for splashing out.

The next night it was dinner at the Mirabelle, London's most famous restaurant. The guests were the amateur riders whose sporting spirits, enjoyment in accepting risks and their great good humour had made it a year of fun and friendship as well as success. It was a grand evening when the food was *the* best, the wine was of the highest class and everyone knew there just was not much better to be had.

The next evening was the most important 'thank you' – it was to the people who had been most involved, those who had really helped – the lads and connexions at the Findon yard. George supplied them all with champagne, got up to speak and told them – with that frankness the Americans are so much less frightened of expressing than the British – just what it had all meant to him. He told them that in this extraordinary year, when his whole life had centred around one driving force – victory in the Championship – it was going to be very hard to adjust back to a normal existence. They were the ones who he would never forget for it was they who had shared the most memorable year in his life. It was with them that he had ridden out every morning, it was they who had become part of his single-minded drive for success. It was worse, too, this farewell to the lads, for while he would be able to keep in touch with most of the friends he had made during the year, to those from the Findon yard who for 10 months had become part of his way of life, this end to the season inevitably meant the end of their close relationship.

Snowy, the wizened old travelling head lad, managed a few words about being a great year and George being a great guy; but the head lad, Ron James, so quick with his wit in the stables could not make the words come out. George Sloan could not cry, he had not since he was seven when he had been taught that it was a 'cissy' failing. Others, however, were feeling close to it, they knew they had been part of a unique year, and fun though it was to drink champagne, to wallow in the success, it was even sadder that it was all over.

The next stop was Nick Henderson's wedding in Warwickshire where the young farmer, John Phillips, asked George whether he had ever slid down a tent pole. Apparently that was a new area of devilment to George, who asked for a demonstration. John and he climbed up the outside of the tent but the demonstrator claimed the hole was too small for him. George was persuaded to take over, slid a few feet before getting caught up on a hook used to hold flowerpots. The startled band stopped playing and the partygoers turned to watch. He remained stationary for just a few seconds before the trousers gave way and there was a noise of ripping cloth, as he hurtled to the ground. He had established himself in yet another county as a mischief-maker; but he did think that, on this occasion, the position of the rip in his apparel entailed a swift retreat upstairs to bed.

George crept back to Sussex the next day. A whole week of celebrations was takings its toll; sleep now seemed more important than the feeling of elation, but there was still one party to go. The most important keg in the campaign, his trainer Josh Gifford, was giving him a farewell dinner. Toasts were drunk to the trainer and the champion but everyone knew that they had a great deal more to thank each other for than these formal achnowledgements could suggest. Both had played important roles in each other's successes, in a season when Josh had left the ranks of 'promising trainers' to join the 'top trainers', and George had achieved his great ambition.

But now it was all over: George flew off the next day laden with memories, trophies, baggage and two Jack Russell puppies. Ahead lay more celebrating and a formidable amount of work. The Cosmopolitan Spas had boomed during their year of unusual management but only on the basis of non-expansionary policy. To make the money he needed to buy Grand National horses, to build up the Hillsboro Hounds, his American racing stables as well as his home, he had to apply the same determination and dedication to the business as he had in the race for the Championship.

There were, too, some more debts of gratitude to settle – especially those owed to the Americans who had backed his venture with financial and moral support. The 'thank you' took the form of an elegant and formal dinner at his Southern Colonial style home, Panorama Farm, high on a hilltop in Middle Tennessee with the evening temperature well into the 90s, the guests drank their toasts to a wonderful year with his Championship prize – vintage champagne presented by Bollinger, which had arrived the day before by special express delivery.

Bollinger's most publicized prize is not the dozen crates of champagne they give to both the Amateur and Professional Champions, but the awards dinner which they stage in the jockey's honour. Invitations to this dinner are prizes in themselves for the top contributors to National Hunt racing – the leading jockeys, trainers, owners and journalists.

Winners of The Bollinger Trophies

Champion Jockeys

1963–1964 .. J. Gifford
1964–1965 .. T. W. Biddlecombe
1965–1966 .. T. W. Biddlecombe
1966–1967 .. J. Gifford
1967–1968 .. J. Gifford
1968–1969 { T. W. Biddlecombe / B. R. Davies
1969–1970 .. B. R. Davies
1970–1971 .. G. Thorner
1971–1972 .. B. R. Davies
1972–1973 .. R. E. Barry
1973–1974 .. R. E. Barry
1974–1975 .. T. Stack
1975–1976 .. J. Francome
1976–1977 .. T. Stack
1977–1978 .. J. J. O'Neill

Leading Amateur Riders

1963–1964 .. S. Davenport
1964–1965 .. M. C. Gifford
1965–1966 .. C. D. Collins
1966–1967 .. C. D. Collins
1967–1968 .. R. Tate
1960–1969 .. R. Tate
1969–1970 .. M. W. Dickinson
1970–1971 .. The Hon. J. Lawrence
1971–1972 .. C. W. Foulkes
1972–1973 .. R. J. Smith
1973–1974 .. A. Webber
1974–1975 .. R. Lamb
1975 1976 { P. Greenall / G. Jones
1976–1977 .. P. Greenall
1977–1978 .. G. Sloan

Guest Speakers

1964 .. Field Marshal The Lord Harding
1965 .. The Lord Willoughby de Broke
1966 .. The Viscount Leverhulme
1967 .. Captain M. H. Gosling
1968 .. Sir Alec Douglas Home, Bart., M.P.
1969 .. The Lord Wigg
1970 .. Edward Courage
1971 .. The Lord Oaksey
1972 .. Clive Graham
1973 .. Clement Freud, M.P.
1974 .. Christopher Collins
1975 .. The Lord Mancroft
1976 .. Harry Thomson Jones
1977 .. The Lord Kilmany
1978 .. Sir Timothy Kitson, M.P.

Jonjo O'Neill

George Sloan

The 16th Bollinger Trophy Dinner

at

VINTNERS HALL

on

Monday, 11th December, 1978

The Champions are judged by their speeches which are seized on by the press and racing powers. George started his with a dash of humour and finished with an appreciation which made the élite band of listeners – pleasantly mulled by Bollinger's high-class wine supply – sit up and become conscious of what so many took for granted. They could be proud of their unusual world – the domain of National Hunt for here the British were the best, and here that sadly rarer and rarer competitive but sporting spirit still flourished.

'English steeplechasing sets the standard for the world. You, as officials, owners, trainers, jockeys and enthusiasts are the custodians of this sport for future generations. You have the responsibility of promoting, building, and improving it, so that those in the future will have the opportunity to experience the sweet spice of competition and cameraderie that each of us has been fortunate enough to find. I shall never forget this past year and will forever cherish the many friendships that have come and continue to come from that experience.

'I would like to express my heartfelt appreciation to all those who have made my English adventure so meaningful – from The Queen Mother who has so graciously supported steeplechasing and has been so hospitable to me; to the officials who, although sometimes in error, make the judgements and decisions that must be made to direct the sport; to trainers and jockeys who put their whole self and life into the game; to the fans and punters upon whom steeplechasing ultimately depends and who give such grand support.

'Charles Kingsley expressed my feeling so well when he wrote:

> Can we forget one friend? can we forget one face?
> Which cheered us toward our end, which nerved us for our race?
> One presence which has made us know
> To God – like souls how deep our debt,
> We would not, if we could, – forget'